Easy

CASSEROLES

COOKBOOK

Simple Recipes

for Convenient Meals & Side Dishes

Barbara C. Jones

Easy Casseroles Cookbook

1st Printing   March 2006

ISBN 1-931294-84-4 Paper Edition
Library of Congress Number:
200411 2393

Illustrated by Nancy Murphy Griffith
Printed in USA
Edited, Designed and Published in the
United States of America
by Cookbook Resources, LLC
541 Doubletree Drive
Highland Village, Texas 75077
Toll free 866-229-2665
www.cookbookresources.com

cookbook
resources LLC

Introduction

Recipes in **Easy Casseroles** are mostly family recipes that are easy enough for everyday, but nice enough for company and friends for weekend entertaining. These dishes are great for potlucks, new neighbors, church suppers, supper clubs and fun socials.

They are easy recipes because they don't require lots of preparation time or special ingredients. You probably have all the ingredients in your kitchen already, but if you have to go to the grocery store, the ingredients are easy to find.

They are also versatile, colorful and sometimes modern adaptations of old family recipes many of us enjoyed in our early years. And they are tasty and delicious enough to be modern family classics. They are the meals that kids and parents request over and over and become favorite food memories.

And Salads Too...As an added addition to our outstanding casserole recipes, we have added several great salad recipes that are new, different and a little out of the ordinary. They are tasty accompaniments to our casseroles and make any meal complete.

We hope you enjoy this wonderful collection of everyday and entertaining recipes that will make your life easier and your diners as happy as can be.

Enjoy!

Barbara C. Jones

Contents

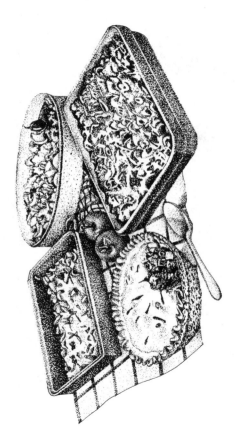

CASSEROLE DISH SIZES

Choosing casserole dishes today is lots of fun, but may be a little confusing because there are so many different shapes and sizes. Listed below are the most common sizes, but don't hesitate to try a beautiful dish with a lid and handles that would look great on your table.

One of the best things about casseroles is that you serve the recipe in the same dish you cooked it in. If the dish has handles, it makes serving much easier and the clean-up is limited. If you only have 1 casserole or baking dish, your best bet is probably the 13 x 9 x 2-inch baking dish. Most of the casseroles in this book work with this dish. We've also listed several casseroles that are big enough, you can make 2 smaller casseroles and freeze one for a later date.

Dish Sizes	Approximate Volume
8 x 8 x 2 square	8 cups
11 x 7 x 2 rectangular	8 cups
9 x 9 x 2 rectangular	10 cups
13 x 9 x 2 rectangular	15 cups
1-quart casserole	4 cups
2-quart casserole	8 cups
2 1/2-quart casserole	10 cups
3-quart casserole	12 cups

Casserole Freezing Tips

The best way to save time and money is to make a large casserole, put it into 2 smaller dishes and freeze 1 for another day. When you have an extra casserole in the freezer, you'll never be caught without a meal ready to go. Freezing suggestions are listed with most of the recipes in this cookbook. Here are a few more helpful tips for freezing casseroles.

1. Always let casserole cool before freezing.
2. Reduce cooking time of casserole by 10 to 20 minutes, so it will not dry out when it is reheated.
3. Always cover the casserole before putting it in the freezer.
4. If the final ingredients are added to the top of the casserole for added "crunch" (potato chips, fried onion rings), don't freeze them, but wait to add them when you reheat it.
5. Use an oven-to-freezer container so you don't have to change dishes.
6. Reduce the seasonings slightly because they may intensify with time.
7. Store in freezer no more than 2 to 4 weeks to maintain freshness and moisture.
9. Defrost in refrigerator.

Brunch

An Apple for Breakfast

This is a really neat breakfast casserole to go along with your "bacon and eggs" and a delicious way to serve fruit with breakfast or brunch!

4-5 tart cooking apples, peeled, sliced	
3/4 cup chopped pecans	180 ml
1/2 cup golden raisins	120 ml
6 tablespoons brown sugar	90 ml
1/2 teaspoon cinnamon	2 ml
1/4 cup (1/2 stick) butter	60 ml
6 eggs	
1 1/2 cups orange juice	360 ml
1 cup flour	240 ml
3 tablespoons sugar	45 ml
Maple syrup	

• Saute apples, pecans, raisins, brown sugar, cinnamon and butter in large skillet, until apples begin to soften, about 6 minutes, and stir often.

• Place in buttered 9 x 13 (23 x 33 cm) inch baking dish.

• In mixing bowl, combine eggs, orange juice, flour and 3/4 teaspoon (4 ml) salt, beat slowly until mixture is smooth and stir around edges of bowl.

• Pour over apple mixture. Sprinkle with sugar and a little cinnamon.

• Bake uncovered at 400° (204° C) for about 20 to 25 minutes or until knife inserted in center comes out clean. Serve with maple syrup.

Breakfast Tortillas

¾ cup chopped onion	180 ml
¼ cup (½ stick) butter	60 ml
¼ cup flour	60 ml
¾ cup milk	180 ml
1 pint half-and-half cream	.5 kg
1 (7 ounce) can chopped green chilies	198 g
10 eggs	
3 avocados	
8 (8-inch) flour tortillas	8 (20 cm)
1 (8 ounce) package shredded Monterey Jack cheese	227 g

- Saute onion in butter in large skillet. Stir in flour and cook on low 1 minute and stir constantly. Add milk and cream and cook on medium heat and stir constantly, until mixture thickens. Add green chilies, 1 teaspoon (5 ml) salt and garlic powder. Remove sauce from heat and set aside.

- In another skillet, scramble eggs lightly and remove from heat.

- Mash avocados and sprinkle with a little salt.

- Spread tortillas on counter and dip 2 tablespoons (30 ml) sauce, one-eighth of the eggs and one-eighth of avocados on each tortilla.

- Roll and place seam-side down on greased 9 x 13-inch (23 x 33 cm) baking dish. Pour remaining sauce over tortillas.

- Bake covered at 325° (162° C) for about 25 minutes or just until tortillas are hot and bubbly.

- Remove from oven, sprinkle cheese over top and return to oven for about 10 minutes.

Tip: To remove tortillas from baking pan, always use a long, wide spatula so the tortillas do not break up.

Brunch

Breakfast Bake

1 pound hot sausage, cooked, crumbled	.5 kg
2 tablespoons dried onion flakes	30 ml
1 cup shredded cheddar cheese	240 ml
1 cup biscuit mix	240 ml
5 eggs	
2 cups milk	480 ml

- Place cooked, crumbled sausage in sprayed 9 x 13-inch (23 x 33 cm) baking dish. Sprinkle with onion flakes and cheese.

- Combine biscuit mix, eggs and a little salt and pepper in mixing bowl. Beat well with fork (not mixer). Add milk, stir until fairly smooth and pour over sausage mixture.

- Bake covered for 35 minutes.

Tip: To use this recipe for a brunch or morning bridge club, just add 1 (8 ounce/227 g) can whole kernel corn, drained, to make it a little heartier.

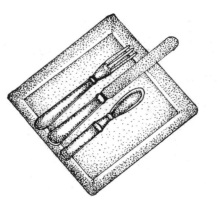

Overnight Breakfast

*This is "French toast" the easy way and it's not just
for company! The kids will love it too.*

7 cups small cubed French bread,		
bottom crust removed		1.6 ml
¾ cup chopped pecans		180 ml
1 (3 ounce) package cream cheese, softened		84 g
4 tablespoons sugar		60 ml
1 (8 ounce) carton whipping cream		227 g
½ cup real maple syrup		120 ml
6 eggs, slightly beaten		
1 teaspoon vanilla		5 ml
½ teaspoon ground cinnamon		2 ml

• Place cubed bread in greased 9 x 13-inch (23 x 33 cm) baking dish and press down gently. Sprinkle with pecans.

• In mixing bowl, beat cream cheese and sugar until fluffy and gradually mix in whipping cream and syrup.

• Whisk eggs, vanilla, cinnamon and a little salt in separate bowl and fold into cream cheese-whipping cream mixture. Slowly pour this mixture evenly over bread.

• Cover and refrigerate overnight.

• Remove from refrigerator 20 minutes before baking.

• Bake covered at 350° (176° C) for 30 minutes or until center sets and top is golden brown. To serve, cut into squares and serve with maple syrup.

Quick Breakfast Sandwiches

8 slices white bread*	
Butter, softened	
2 cups cooked, finely chopped ham	480 ml
1 cup shredded Swiss cheese	240 ml
3 eggs, beaten	
1⅓ cups milk	
1 tablespoon dried, minced onion flakes	400 ml
1 teaspoon prepared mustard	15 ml
	5 ml

• Trim crusts off bread slices. Spread butter on 1 side of each slice of bread. Place 4 slices in buttered 8-inch (20 cm) square baking pan.

• Top bread slices with chopped ham and remaining bread slices, buttered side up. Sprinkle with shredded Swiss cheese.

• Combine eggs, milk, onion flakes, prepared mustard with a little salt and mix well. Slowly pour over bread slices. Cover and refrigerate overnight or at least 8 hours.

• Remove baking pan from refrigerator about 10 minutes before cooking. Bake uncovered at 325° (162° C) for 30 minutes or until center sets. To serve, cut into 4 sandwiches.

Tip: Use regular bread slices, not thin sandwich slices.

Elegant Eggs

¼ cup plus	60 ml
2 tablespoons butter	30 ml
6 tablespoons flour	90 ml
2 teaspoons dried dill weed	10 ml
½ cup dry white wine	120 ml
½ cup clam juice	120 ml
1½ cups whipping cream	360 ml
1¼ cups grated parmesan cheese	300 ml
14 hard-boiled eggs	
2 (6 ounce) cans shrimp, drained, veined	2 (168 g)
1½ cups dry breadcrumbs	360 ml
1 teaspoon Creole seasoning	5 ml

• Melt ¼ cup (60 ml) butter in saucepan and stir in flour and dill weed. Cook on medium heat for about 2 minutes, but do not brown.

• Stir in wine, clam juice and cream and cook, stirring constantly, until sauce thickens. Stir in parmesan cheese and set aside.

• Cut eggs in half lengthwise and place eggs, yolk side up, in buttered, shallow baking dish.

• Cover with shrimp and pour sauce over top of shrimp.

• Melt 2 tablespoons (30 ml) butter. Combine breadcrumbs, Creole seasoning and melted butter. Sprinkle on top of sauce-covered with shrimp. Let stand at room temperature for 30 minutes.

• Bake uncovered at 375° (190° C) for 20 minutes or until casserole is hot and bubbly.

Fiesta Eggs

1 pound sausage	.5 kg
½ green, ½ red bell pepper, chopped	
3 green onions, chopped	
1 (10 ounce) can tomatoes and green chilies	280 g
½ cup hot, chunky salsa	120 ml
4 ounces cubed processed cheese	114 g
10 eggs, slightly beaten	
½ cup sour cream	120 ml
⅔ cup milk	160 ml

• Slowly brown sausage, bell peppers and onions in skillet and drain.

• Dry skillet with paper towels. Pour tomatoes and green chilies, salsa and processed cheese in skillet and cook. Stir constantly, only until cheese melts. Remove from heat.

• In bowl beat eggs, 1½ teaspoons (7 ml) salt, sour cream and milk and fold in sausage mixture and tomato-cheese mixture. Transfer to greased 7 x 11-inch (18 x 28 cm) baking dish.

• Bake uncovered at 325° (162° C) for about 25 minutes or until center sets.

Bacon & Eggs Anyone?

This casserole is also great for a late-night supper. You really don't need anything else with it except biscuits or toast.

2 potatoes, peeled, cubed	
¼ cup (½ stick)	60 ml
plus 3 tablespoons butter	45 ml
¼ cup flour	60 ml
1 pint half-and-half cream	.5 kg
1 (16 ounce) package shredded cheddar cheese	.5 kg
1 teaspoon Italian seasoning	5 ml
12 hard-boiled eggs, sliced	
1 pound bacon, cooked, slightly crumbled	.5 kg
1½ cups breadcrumbs	360 ml

• Cook potatoes in salted water just until tender, but do not overcook. Drain well.

• In large saucepan melt ¼ cup (60 ml) butter and stir in flour. Cook, stirring constantly, 1 minute or until smooth.

• Gradually add cream and cook over medium heat, stirring constantly, until sauce thickens.

• Add cheddar cheese, Italian seasoning, ½ teaspoon (2 ml) each of salt and pepper to taste, stirring constantly, until cheese melts. Remove from heat.

• In buttered 9 x 13-inch (23 x 33 cm) baking dish, layer half of egg slices, half of bacon and half of cheese sauce.

• Spoon potatoes over cheese sauce and top with remaining egg slices, bacon and cheese sauce. Melt 3 tablespoons (45 ml) butter and combine with breadcrumbs. Sprinkle over top of casserole.

• Cover and refrigerate overnight.

• Before baking remove casserole from refrigerator and let stand for about 20 minutes. Uncover and bake at 350° (176° C) for 30 minutes.

Baked-Stuffed Eggs

6 hard-boiled eggs	
1/2 cup fresh very finely chopped mushrooms caps	
3 tablespoons butter	120 ml
1 tablespoon white wine Worcestershire sauce	45 ml
2-3 dashes hot sauce	15 ml

- Split eggs lengthwise. Remove yolks, set whites aside and mash yolks.

- Saute mushrooms in butter. Add mushrooms and seasonings to yolks and mix well.

- Stuff into egg-white shells and arrange in buttered, shallow baking dish.

Cheese Sauce:

3 tablespoons butter	45 ml
3 tablespoons flour	45 ml
3/4 cup milk	180 ml
2/3 cup shredded cheddar cheese	160 ml
1/2 cup seasoned breadcrumbs	120 ml

- In saucepan, combine butter and flour and cook on medium heat just until butter and flour mix well.

- Add milk slowly and cook, stirring constantly, until mixture is smooth and thick. Remove from heat, fold in cheese and stir until cheese melts.

- Pour cheese sauce over eggs and sprinkle with breadcrumbs.

- Bake uncovered at 350° (176° C) for 20 minutes.

Tortilla Egg Rolls

½ sliced fresh mushrooms	
1 onion, chopped	
½ cup chopped green bell pepper	120 ml
½ cup chopped sweet red bell pepper	120 ml
¼ cup (½ stick) butter	60 ml
6 eggs	
1½ cups half-and-half cream, divided	360 ml
1 cup fully cooked, shredded ham	240 ml
1 (10 ounce) can cream of mushroom soup, divided	280 g
8-10 (8-inch) flour tortillas	8-10 (20 cm)
1½ cups shredded cheddar cheese	360 ml

• Saute mushrooms, onion and both bell peppers in butter and set aside.

• In separate bowl, whisk eggs, ½ cup (120 ml) cream, ham and ¼ teaspoon (1 ml) each of salt and pepper. Pour egg-ham mixture into skillet with mushroom-pepper mixture.

• Cook, stirring constantly, over medium heat until eggs are almost set, but not dry. (Do not overcook eggs.)

• In buttered 9 x 13-inch (23 x 33 cm) baking dish, spread half of soup in baking dish.

• Spread tortillas out on counter and place 3 tablespoons (45 ml) egg-ham mixture in center of each tortilla. Sprinkle each with 1 tablespoon (15 ml) cheese. Roll and place seam-side down over soup.

• Mix remaining soup with 1 cup (240 ml) cream and pour over tortillas.

• Bake covered at 325° (162° C) for about 25 minutes or until tortillas are hot.

• Remove from oven and sprinkle remaining cheese over top of casserole. Return to oven for 5 minutes or until cheese melts.

Sausage Quiche

1 (9-inch) deep-dish uncooked pie shell	23 cm	
1 (7 ounce) can whole green chilies	198 g	
1 pound hot sausage, cooked, crumbled	.5 kg	
4 eggs, slightly beaten		
2 cups half-and-half cream	480 ml	
½ cup grated parmesan cheese	120 ml	
¾ cup grated Swiss cheese	180 ml	

- Line pie shell with split, seeded green chilies. Sprinkle sausage over chilies.

- Combine eggs, cream, both cheeses and about ¼ teaspoon (1 ml) each of salt and pepper. Slowly pour over sausage.

- Cover edge of pastry with thin strip of foil to prevent excessive browning.

- Bake at 350° (176° C) for 35 minutes or until center sets and is golden brown. Allow quiche to set at room temperature for 5 minutes before slicing to serve.

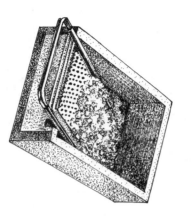

Brunch

Quick Quiche

½ cup (1 stick) butter, melted	120 ml
1½ cups half-and-half cream	360 ml
3 green onions, with tops, chopped	
½ cup biscuit mix	120 ml
1 cup grated Swiss cheese	240 ml
¾ cup chopped ham	180 ml
4 eggs, beaten	

- Grease 10-inch (25 cm) deep pie plate.

- Combine butter, cream, green onions, biscuit mix and ¼ teaspoon (1 ml) each of salt and pepper. Blend well with mixer and pour into pie plate.

- Sprinkle batter with cheese and ham. Push meat below surface with back of spoon.

- Beat eggs in same mixing bowl and pour over ham and cheese.

- Bake at 350° (176° C) for 35 minutes or until center sets.

- Allow to sit at room temperature about 10 minutes before slicing.

Brunch

Quesadilla Pie

1 (4 ounce) can chopped green chilies	114 g
½ pound sausage, cooked, crumbled	227 g
2 cups shredded cheddar cheese	480 ml
3 eggs, well beaten	
1½ cups milk	360 ml
¾ cup biscuit mix	180 ml
Hot salsa	

• Sprinkle green chilies in sprayed 9-inch (23 cm) pie pan. Add layer of cooked sausage and layer of cheddar cheese.

• In separate bowl, combine eggs, milk and biscuit mix and mix well.

• Slowly pour over chilies, sausage and cheese.

• Bake at 350° (176° C) for 35 minutes or until center sets. Serve with salsa on top of each slice.

Tip: To give this "pie" a little more zip, use hot sausage and a few drops of hot sauce!

Chiffon-Cheese Souffle

WOW! Is this ever good. It is light and fluffy, but still very rich. It must be the Old English cheese that gives it that special cheese flavor. This recipe is placed in the Brunch section, but it can easily be served at lunch. It is even good leftover when warmed up.

12 slices white bread, crust removed*	
2 (5 ounce) jars Old English cheese spread, softened	2 (143 g)
6 eggs, beaten	
3 cups milk	710 ml
¾ cup (1½ stick) butter, melted	180 ml

- (Be sure to use a dish with high sides because souffle will rise and fall slightly. The baking dish will be full.)

- Cut each slice of bread into 4 triangles and spoon dab of cheese on each.

- Place triangles evenly in 1 layer in sprayed 9 x 13-inch (23 x 33 cm) baking dish.

- Combine eggs, milk, butter and about ½ teaspoon (2 ml) salt and mix well. Slowly pour mixture over layers of bread.

- Cover and chill 8 hours.

- Remove from refrigerator about 20 minutes before baking.

- Bake uncovered at 350° (176° C) for 1 hour.

Tip: Be sure to use regular slices, not thin slices.

Hot Tamale-Cheese Fiesta

2 (13 ounce) jars beef tamales with sauce	2 (370 g)
1 (10 ounce) can cream of mushroom soup	280 g
2 teaspoons taco seasoning	10 ml
1 (8 ounce) package shredded Mexican 4-cheese blend, divided	227 g

- Drain sauce from tamales into cup and set aside. Put tamales onto plate and remove paper from tamales.

- Place tamales, side by side, in baking dish. Sprinkle one-fourth of cheese over top of tamales.

- Combine ½ cup (120 ml) sauce from tamales, mushroom soup and taco seasoning and mix well.

- Pour sauce mixture over tamales and cheese.

- Bake at 350° (176° C) for 5 to 10 minutes to heat tamales thoroughly.

- Remove from oven and pour one-half of remaining cheese over top and heat until cheese melts.

Cinnamon Souffle

1 loaf cinnamon-raisin bread	
1 (20 ounce) can crushed pineapple, with juice	567 g
1 cup (2 sticks) butter, melted	240 ml
½ cup sugar	120 ml
5 eggs, slightly beaten	
½ cup chopped pecans	120 ml

- Remove very thin crusts from bread. Tear bread into small pieces and place in buttered 9 x 13-inch (23 x 33 cm) baking dish.

- Pour pineapple and juice over bread and set aside. Cream butter and sugar. Add eggs to butter-sugar mixture and mix well.

- Pour creamed mixture over bread and pineapple. Sprinkle chopped pecans over souffle. Bake uncovered at 350° (176° C) for 40 minutes.

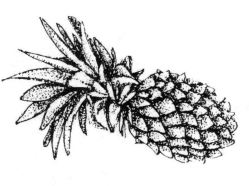

French Toast on the Town

Crisp bacon is a must to serve with this French toast. The only real problem with this recipe is that your weekend guest will come back next weekend for more.

½ cup (1 stick) butter	120 ml
1 cup firmly packed light brown sugar	240 ml
3 tablespoons corn syrup	45 ml
7 slices white bread, crust removed*	
6 eggs, beaten	
1½ cups half-and-half cream	360 ml
½ teaspoon vanilla	2 ml
1 teaspoon almond extract	5 ml
¼ teaspoon ground cinnamon	1 ml

- In saucepan melt butter, add brown sugar and corn syrup, and stir until they blend well.

- Pour mixture into 9 x 13-inch (23 x 33 cm) baking dish. Place bread slices over butter sugar mixture in single layer. (Six slices will fit in baking dish. Cut 1 remaining bread slice to fit around edges of dish.)

- Combine eggs, cream, vanilla, almond extract, cinnamon and ½ teaspoon (2 ml) salt and mix until they blend well. Slowly pour over bread slices. Cover and refrigerate overnight.

- Uncover and bake at 350° (176° C) for about 35 minutes or until golden brown. When serving, cut into squares and lift up with square spatula so brown sugar mixture comes with each serving.

Tip: Be sure to use regular slices and not thin slices.

Sausage-Apple Ring

This is a fun way to serve scrambled eggs and sausage! Your guest will really be impressed! It sounds like a lot of trouble, but it really isn't. You are just doing a lot of flipping.

2 pounds bulk sausage	1 kg
1½ cups crushed cracker crumbs	360 ml
2 eggs, slightly beaten	
½ cup milk	120 ml
¼ cup minced onion	60 ml
1 cup very finely chopped apple	240 ml
Scrambled eggs	

- Thoroughly combine sausage, cracker crumbs, eggs, milk, onion and chopped apple. (This will require a good bit of mixing to get everything worked into sausage.)

- Press into 9-inch (23 cm) ring mold. (Press well because you will have holes in the bottom if sausage is not pressed down well.)

- With knife, ease around top of edge and center edge of ring mold and turn onto shallow baking pan or sheet cake pan with edges.

- Bake at 350° (176° C) for 45 minutes, then drain fat. (The best way I have found to drain fat and to get ring on serving plate is to spoon off fat in center of ring, then take several paper towels and place around ring to absorb fat around edges. Let cool a little.)

- Lay plate, up side down on top of ring. Flip again and your ring center will be ready to be filled with eggs.

- Cover and refrigerate.

- For breakfast the next morning, just reheat ring for about 15 minutes.

- While ring is reheating, scramble about a dozen eggs and fill center of ring.

Green Chili Puff

This recipe is so versatile! You can cut it in little squares and serve warm as an appetizer for brunch or for lunch. And, it goes well with any Mexican meal, morning, noon or night.

10 eggs		
½ cup flour	120 ml	
1 teaspoon baking powder	5 ml	
1 (16 ounce) carton small curd cottage cheese	.5 kg	
1 (8 ounce) package shredded Monterey Jack Cheese	227 g	
1 bunch green onions, with tops, chopped		
1 (8 ounce) package shredded cheddar cheese	227 g	
½ cup (1 stick) butter, melted	120 ml	
1 (7 ounce) can chopped green chilies	198 g	

- Beat eggs in bowl until light and lemon-colored. Add flour, baking powder and ½ teaspoon (2 ml) salt and beat until smooth.

- Add cottage cheese, mozzarella cheese, green onions, cheddar cheese, butter and green chilies. Stir until they mix well.

- Pour into buttered 9 x 13-inch (23 x 33 cm) baking dish.

- Bake uncovered at 350° (176° C) for 40 minutes or until top is slightly brown around edges and center appears firm. Serve immediately. Salsa may be served on the side.

Ranch Sausage and Grits

Can you find a tall, lanky Texan to invite to breakfast? He'll be putty in you hands if you serve him this sausage and grits.

1 cup instant grits	240 ml
1 pound hot sausage	.5 kg
½ teaspoon minced garlic	2 ml
1 (8 ounce) package shredded sharp cheddar cheese, divided	227 g
½ cup hot salsa	120 ml
¼ cup (½ stick) butter, melted	60 ml
2 eggs, beaten	

- Cook instant grits in 2 cups (480 ml) boiling water according to package directions.

- In skillet, brown and cook sausage and garlic and drain.

- Combine cooked grits, sausage, half cheese, salsa, melted butter and eggs and mix well.

- Pour into buttered 9 x 13-inch (23 x 33 cm) baking dish.

- Bake uncovered at 350° (176° C) for 50 minutes. Remove from oven and sprinkle remaining cheese over casserole. Return to oven for 10 minutes.

Curried Fruit Medley

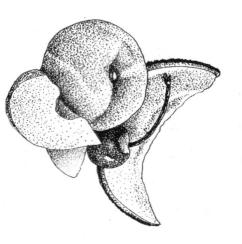

1 (29 ounce) can sliced peaches, drained	805 g
2 (15 ounce) cans pineapple chunks, drained	2 (425 g)
1 (10 ounce) jar maraschino cherries, drained	280 g
1 cup packed brown sugar	240 ml
1 teaspoon curry powder	5 ml
¼ cup (½ stick) butter, sliced	60 ml

• Pour fruit in 9 x 13-inch (23 x 33 cm) baking dish.

• Combine brown sugar and curry and stir well.
  Sprinkle over fruit and dot with butter.

• Bake covered at 350° (176° C) for 30 minutes or until
  is hot and bubbles around edges.

Pineapple-Cheese Casserole

This is really a wonderful and different combination of flavors. It is great served at brunch or great served with a sandwich at lunch.

1 (20 ounce) can pineapple chunks, drained	567 g
1 cup sugar	240 ml
5 tablespoons flour	75 ml
1½ cups shredded cheddar cheese	360 ml
1 stack round, buttery crackers, crushed	
½ cup (1 stick) butter, melted	120 ml

• Butter 9 x 13-inch (23 x 33 cm) baking dish and layer in following order: pineapple, sugar-flour mixture, shredded cheese and cracker crumbs.

• Drizzle melted butter over casserole.

• Bake uncovered at 350° (176° C) for 25 minutes or until bubbly.

Breakfast-Ready Casserole

6 English muffins, halved	
1 pound hot sausage, cooked, drained	.5 kg
1 (8 ounce) package shredded cheddar-jack cheese, divided	227 g
5 eggs, beaten	
1 (10 ounce) can cream of mushroom soup	280 g
2½ cups milk	600 ml

- Line sprayed 9 x 13-inch (23 x 33 cm) baking dish with English-muffin halves and cooked sausage.

- In separate bowl combine half cheese, eggs, soup and milk and mix well.

- Gently pour cheese-soup mixture over sausage and muffins. Sprinkle remaining cheese over top of casserole.

- Bake at 325° (162° C) for 65 to 70 minutes. Test to be sure center of casserole sets.

- Let rest for 10 or 15 minutes before slicing and serving.

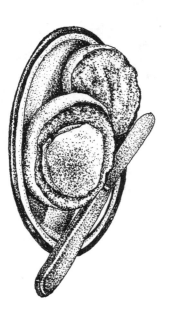

Side Dishes

Spinach-Cheese Manicotti

This does take a little extra time to fill the shells, but it is really a special dish and well worth the time it takes!

1 onion, minced	
2 teaspoons minced garlic	10 ml
1 (15 ounce) carton ricotta cheese	425 g
1 (3 ounce) package cream cheese, softened	84 g
1 (8 ounce) package shredded mozzarella cheese, divided	227 g
1 (3 ounce) package grated parmesan cheese, divided	84 g
2 teaspoons Italian seasoning	10 ml
1 (10 ounce) box frozen chopped spinach, thawed, drained	280 g
9 manicotti shells, cooked	
1 (26 ounce) jar spaghetti sauce	737 g

• Saute onion and garlic in a little oil in skillet and set aside.

• In mixing bowl, combine ricotta, cream cheese, half mozzarella, half parmesan cheese, Italian seasoning, ½ teaspoon (2 ml) each of salt and pepper and beat until they mix well.

• Drain spinach with several paper towels and squeeze until spinach drains well. Add spinach and onion to cheese mixture and mix well.

• Spoon this mixture into manicotti shells 1 teaspoon (5 ml) at a time. (Be careful not to tear shells.)

• Pour half of spaghetti sauce in bottom of greased 9 x 13-inch (23 x 33 cm) baking dish. Arrange shells over sauce and top with remaining sauce.

• Cover and bake at 350° (176° C) for 30 minutes. Remove from oven, uncover and sprinkle remaining cheeses over top. Return to oven just until cheese melts.

Confetti Orzo

This is really good. The alfredo sauce gives it a very mild, pleasing flavor. (Sure beats "buttered rice")

8 ounces orzo pasta	227 g
½ cup (1 stick) butter	120 ml
3 cups broccoli florets, stemmed	710 ml
1 bunch green onions, with tops, chopped	
1 sweet red bell pepper, seeded, chopped	
2 cups celery, chopped	480 ml
1 clove garlic, minced	
½ teaspoon cumin	2 ml
2 teaspoons chicken bouillon	10 ml
1 (8 ounce) carton sour cream	227 g
1 (16 ounce) jar creamy alfredo sauce	.5 kg

- Cook orzo according to package directions, however, it is best to stir orzo several times during cooking time. Drain.

- While orzo is cooking, melt butter in skillet and saute broccoli, onions, red bell pepper, celery, garlic and cumin and cook just until tender-crisp.

- Add chicken bouillon to vegetables.

- Spoon into large bowl and fold in sour cream, alfredo sauce, 1 teaspoon (5 ml) each of salt and pepper and orzo. Spoon into buttered 9 x 13-inch (23 x 33 cm) baking dish.

- This is ready to cook, but you may refrigerate it and cook later. After it has come to room temperature, cook covered at 325° (162° C) for 30 minutes.

Tip: This can easily be made into a main dish by adding 3-4 cups (1 L) chopped, cooked chicken or turkey.

Carnival Couscous

Take a back seat rice! Couscous is here!

1 (6 ounce) box herbed-chicken couscous	168 g	
¼ cup (½ stick) butter	60 ml	
1 sweet red bell pepper, minced		
1 yellow squash, seeded, minced		
1 cup fresh broccoli florets, finely chopped	240 ml	
1 cup celery, chopped	240 ml	

• Cook couscous according to package directions, but omit butter called for on box.

• With butter in saucepan, saute bell pepper, squash, broccoli and celery and cook about 10 minutes or until vegetables are almost tender.

• Combine couscous, vegetables and ½ teaspoon (2 ml) each of salt and pepper and serve.

Tip: *If you want to make this in advance, place couscous and vegetables in buttered baking dish and mix well. Bake covered at 325° (162° C) for about 20 minutes.*

Couscous is an ideal side dish for any entree because it absorbs flavors as it soaks up liquid. Couscous is a fine, tiny, round Middle Eastern pasta that is often thought of as a grain.

Curried Couscous

1½ cups chicken broth	360 ml
½ cup golden raisins	120 ml
1 teaspoon curry powder	5 ml
1 cup uncooked couscous	240 ml
⅓ cup oil	80 ml
2 tablespoons lemon juice	30 ml
1 teaspoon sugar	5 ml
½ cup slivered almonds, toasted	120 ml
2 fresh green onions, sliced	

- In saucepan, combine chicken broth, raisins, curry powder and ½ teaspoon (2 ml) salt and bring to a boil.

- Remove from heat and let stand 5 minutes. Fluff with fork and cook, uncovered.

- Combine oil, lemon juice, sugar and almonds and toss with couscous.

- Sprinkle green onion over top and serve.

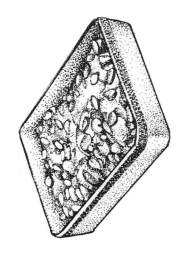

Sensational Spaghetti

Forget the tomato sauce. This is spaghetti to love!

½ cup (1 stick) butter	120 ml
1½ teaspoons minced garlic	7 ml
1 (12 ounce) package thin spaghetti	340 g
1 cup grated parmesan cheese	240 ml
1 pint whipping cream	.5 kg
1 teaspoon dried parsley flakes	5 ml
10-12 strips bacon, fried crisp, crumbled	

• Melt butter and saute garlic in large skillet until slightly brown. Cook spaghetti according to package directions and drain.

• Add spaghetti, parmesan cheese, cream, parsley flakes, and ½ teaspoon (2 ml) each of salt and pepper and mix well.

• Spoon into buttered 2-quart (2 L) baking dish. Cover and bake at 325° (162° C) just until warm, about 15 minutes.

• Uncover and sprinkle crumbled bacon over casserole.

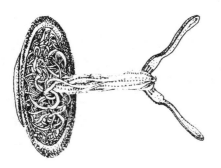

Pasta Frittata

It is a great dish for a luncheon or late night supper.

1 onion, chopped
1 green bell pepper, chopped
1 sweet red bell pepper, chopped
2 tablespoons (¼ stick) butter   30 ml
1 (7 ounce) box thin spaghetti, slightly broken,
      cooked   198 g
1 (8 ounce) package shredded mozzarella
      cheese   227 g
5 eggs
1 cup milk   240 ml
⅓ cup shredded parmesan cheese   80 ml
1 tablespoon dried basil   15 ml
1 teaspoon oregano   5 ml

• In skillet, saute onion and both peppers in butter over
   medium heat for about 5 minutes, but do not brown.

• In large bowl combine onion-pepper mixture and
   spaghetti and toss. Add mozzarella cheese and toss.

• In separate bowl, beat eggs, milk, parmesan cheese,
   basil, oregano, ½ teaspoon (2 ml) each of salt and
   pepper. Add spaghetti mixture and pour into
   buttered 9 x 13-inch (23 x 33 cm) baking dish.

• Cover with foil and bake at 375° (190° C) for about
   15 to 20 minutes. Uncover and make sure eggs are
   set. If not, bake 2 to 3 minutes longer.

Tip: This can be put together, refrigerated and baked later. Let it get
to roomtemperature before placing in oven. Cut into squares to
serve.

Mushroom Pasta

1 onion, chopped	
1 cup celery, chopped	240 ml
1 green and 1 red bell pepper, chopped	
6 tablespoons (¾ stick) butter	90 ml
1⅓ cups orzo pasta	320 ml
1 (14 ounce) can beef broth	396 g
1 (7 ounce) can sliced mushrooms, drained	198 g
1 tablespoon Worcestershire sauce	15 ml
¾ cup chopped walnuts	180 ml
Chopped green onions for garnish	

- Saute onion, celery, bell pepper in butter.

- Cook orzo in beef broth and 1 cup (240 ml) water for 10 to 11 minutes and drain.

- In large bowl, combine onion-bell pepper mixture, orzo, mushrooms, Worcestershire, walnuts and ½ teaspoon (2 ml) each of salt and pepper and mix well.

- Transfer to buttered 2-quart (2 L) baking dish and bake covered at 325° (162° C) for 30 minutes.

- When ready to serve, sprinkle chopped green onions over top of casserole.

Squash Dressing

2 (6 ounce) packages Mexican cornbread mix	2 (168 g)
2 eggs	
1⅓ cups milk	320 ml
2 pounds yellow squash, sliced	1 kg
½ cup (1 stick) butter	120 ml
1 cup onion, chopped	240 ml
1 cup celery, chopped	240 ml
½ cup green bell pepper, chopped	120 ml
1 (10 ounce) can condensed cream of chicken soup	280 g
2 teaspoons chicken bouillon	10 ml

• Prepare cornbread according to package directions with eggs and milk. Cool and crumble into large bowl.

• Combine squash and 1 cup (240 ml) water in saucepan and bring to a boil. Cook about 10 minutes until squash is tender. Drain and mash.

• Melt butter in skillet over medium heat and saute onion, celery and bell pepper.

• Combine crumbled cornbread, squash, onion mixture, cream of chicken soup, milk and chicken bouillon. Mix well and spoon into greased 9 x 13-inch (23 x 33 cm) baking dish.

• Bake uncovered at 350° (176° C) for 45 minutes.

Eggplant Frittata

This is a delicious way to serve eggplant for a light lunch and it is rich enough to be served as the main course. You could put it together the day before the lunch, then cook just before serving.

3 cups peeled, finely chopped eggplant	710 ml
½ cup green bell pepper, chopped	120 ml
3 tablespoons extra light olive oil	45 ml
1 (8 ounce) jar roasted red peppers, drained, chopped	227 g
10 eggs	
½ cup half-and-half cream	120 ml
1 teaspoon Italian seasoning	5 ml
⅓ cup grated parmesan cheese	80 ml

- Cook eggplant and bell pepper in oil in skillet for 2 to 3 minutes, just until tender. Stir in roasted red peppers.

- In mixing bowl, combine eggs, cream, 1 teaspoon salt (5 ml), Italian seasoning and ¼ teaspoon (1 ml) pepper and beat just until they blend well.

- Add eggplant-pepper mixture to egg-cream mixture. Pour into buttered 10-inch (25 cm) pie plate.

- Bake covered 325° (162° C) for about 15 minutes or until center sets.

- Uncover and sprinkle parmesan cheese over top. Return to oven for about 5 minutes, just until cheese melts slightly.

- Cut into wedges to serve.

Creamy Macaroni and Cheese

Yes, this is more trouble than opening that "blue box", but it is well worth the time to make this macaroni and cheese.

1 (12 ounce) package macaroni	340 g
6 tablespoons (³/4 stick) butter	90 ml
¼ cup flour	60 ml
2 cups milk	480 ml
1 (1 pound) package cubed processed cheese	.5 kg

• Cook macaroni according to package directions and drain.

• Melt butter in saucepan and stir in flour, ½ teaspoon (2 ml) each of salt and pepper until they blend well.

• Slowly add milk, stirring constantly, and heat until it begins to thicken. Add cheese and stir until cheese melts.

• Pour cheese sauce over macaroni and mix well.

• Pour into buttered 2½-quart (2.5 L) baking dish. Bake covered at 350° (176° C) for 30 minutes or until bubbly.

Unforgettable Tortellini Bake

1 (18 ounce) package frozen cheese tortellini, cooked, drained   510 g

1 (16 ounce) package frozen chopped broccoli, thawed, drained   .5 kg

1 (4 ounce) jar diced pimentos   114 g

½ cup chopped onion   120 ml

1 clove garlic, minced

2 tablespoons butter   30 ml

2 tablespoons flour   30 ml

1 teaspoon Italian seasoning   5 ml

⅛ teaspoon ground nutmeg   .5 ml

1 cup half-and-half cream   240 ml

⅓ cup grated parmesan cheese   80 ml

½ cup shredded mozzarella cheese   120 ml

- Combine tortellini, broccolli and pimentos in large bowl and set aside.

- Saute onion and garlic in butter in saucepan. Over medium heat, stir in flour, ½ teaspoon (2 ml) each of salt, seasonsed salt (if you have it) and pepper, Italian seasoning and nutmeg and mix well. Gradually stir in cream until mixture blends well. Cook, stirring constantly, until sauce thickens.

- Fold in parmesan cheese and stir until cheese melts. Fold in tortellini-broccoli mixture. Spoon into greased 2½-quart (2.5 L) baking dish.

- Bake covered at 350° (176° C) for 45 minutes or until hot and bubbly.

- Remove from oven and sprinkle mozzarella cheese over top of casserole. Return to oven for 5 minutes or until cheese melts.

Artichoke Squares

These artichoke squares are perfect for a brunch because they can be served hot or at room temperature.

2 (6 ounce) jars marinated artichoke hearts, with liquid	2 (168 g)
1 onion, finely chopped	
½ teaspoon minced garlic	2 ml
4 eggs, beaten	
⅓ cup breadcrumbs	80 ml
1 (8 ounce) package cheddar cheese	227 g
1 tablespoon dried parsley flakes	15 ml

• Drain liquid (marinade) from 1 jar artichoke hearts in skillet, heat and saute onion and garlic. (Discard remaining 1 jar artichoke marinade.)

• Chop artichoke hearts and set aside.

• In separate bowl, combine eggs, breadcrumbs, ¼ teaspoon (1 ml) each of salt and pepper.

• Fold in cheese and parsley. Add artichokes and onions and mix well.

• Spoon into greased 9-inch (23 cm) square baking dish.

• Bake uncovered at 325° (162° C) for 30 minutes. Allow several minutes before cutting into squares to serve.

Tip: This recipe can be made ahead of time and reheated when ready to serve.

Emerald Rice

2 (10 ounce) boxes frozen chopped spinach, thawed, well drained	2 (280 g)
1½ cups cooked rice	360 ml
1 (8 ounce) package shredded cheddar cheese	227 g
3 eggs, beaten	
1 (5 ounce) can evaporated milk	143 g
3 tablespoons finely chopped onion	45 ml
2 tablespoons (¼ stick) butter, melted	30 ml
1 teaspoon chicken bouillon	5 ml
¼ teaspoon dried thyme	1 ml
⅛ teaspoon ground nutmeg	.5 ml

- Cook spinach according to package directions and drain very well.

- Stir in cooked rice and cheddar cheese.

- In separate bowl, combine eggs and evaporated milk and heat until they blend well.

- Add onion, butter, 1 teaspoon salt (5 ml), bouillon, thyme and nutmeg and mix well.

- Transfer to greased 2-quart (2 L) baking dish. Cover and bake at 350° (176° C) for 20 minutes.

- Uncover and continue baking for another 20 minutes or until knife inserted in center comes out clean.

Not Just Buttered Rice

1 cup uncooked white rice	240 ml
6 tablespoons (³/₄ stick) butter, melted	90 ml
1 teaspoon garlic powder	5 ml
¼ cup dried parsley flakes	60 ml
1 onion, finely chopped	
1 egg, beaten	
1 (16 ounce) box cubed jalapeno	
processed cheese	.5 kg
1 cup milk	240 ml

• In large bowl, combine rice, 1½ cups (360 ml) water, melted butter, ½ teaspoon (2 ml) each of salt and pepper, garlic powder, parsley, onion and egg and mix well.

• In saucepan, combine cheese and milk and heat, stirring constantly, until cheese melts.

• Stir into rice-egg mixture. Spoon into buttered 3-quart (3 L) baking dish.

• Bake covered at 350° (176° C) for 60 minutes. This can be cooked, frozen and reheated later.

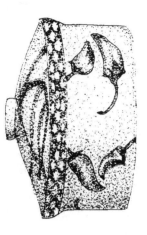

A Different Stuffing

1 (6 ounce) package long grain, wild rice ... 168 g
¼ cup (½ stick) butter ... 60 ml
1½ cups celery, chopped ... 360 ml
1 onion, chopped
1 sweet red bell pepper, finely chopped
1 small carrot, finely grated
¾ cup chopped walnuts ... 180 ml
⅛ teaspoon cayenne pepper ... .5 ml
1 (6 ounce) box chicken stuffing mix ... 168 g
1 egg
1 cup chicken broth ... 240 ml

• Prepare rice according to package directions.

• Melt butter in skillet and saute celery, onion, bell pepper, carrot and walnuts. Stir in cayenne pepper.

• Prepare chicken stuffing according to package directions.

• In large bowl, combine rice, celery-carrot mixture, egg and prepared stuffing mix.

• Fold in broth and spoon into buttered 3-quart (3 L) baking dish.

• Cover and bake at 350° (176° C) for 35 minutes.

Red and Green Wild Rice

You have rice and vegetables all in one delicious dish - and besides that, you have color and character!

1 (6 ounce) package long grain, wild rice   168 g
1 sweet, red bell pepper, julienned
2 small zucchini, julienned
2 stalks fresh broccoli cut into bite-size pieces
½ head cauliflower, cut into bite-size pieces
½ cup (1 stick) butter, melted   120 ml
1 teaspoon dried sweet basil   5 ml
½ cup slivered almonds   120 ml
1 (8 ounce) package shredded cheddar cheese   227 g

• Cook rice according to package directions and set aside.

• In large-size bowl, combine bell pepper, zucchini, broccoli and cauliflower. Cover with wax paper and microwave 3 minutes. Turn bowl and stir the vegetables. Microwave 2 more minutes.

• Add melted butter, 1 teaspoon (5 ml) each of salt and pepper, basil, almonds and rice and toss together.

• Spoon into buttered 9 x 13-inch (23 x 33 cm) baking dish.

• Bake covered at 350° (176° C) for about 20 minutes or until heated thoroughly.

• Just before serving, sprinkle cheese over top and return to oven for 5 minutes.

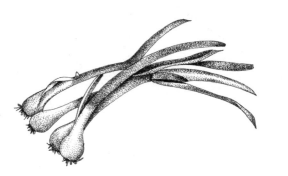

Side Dishes

Creamy Rice Bake

1 cup finely chopped green onions, with tops	240 ml
¼ cup (½ stick) butter	60 ml
3 cups cooked instant white rice	710 ml
1 (8 ounce) carton sour cream	227 g
¾ cup small curd cottage cheese	180 ml
1¼ cups Monterey Jack cheese	300 ml

- Saute onion in butter in large skillet.

- Remove from heat and add rice, sour cream, cottage cheese, ½ teaspoon (2 ml) each of salt and pepper and Monterey Jack cheese.

- Toss lightly to mix and spoon into greased 2-quart (2 L) baking dish.

- Bake covered at 350° (176° C) for 35 minutes.

Italian Bake

1 pound Italian sausage links, sliced	.5 kg
3 cups fresh sliced mushrooms	710 ml
1 onion, chopped	
1 green bell pepper, chopped	
1 teaspoon minced garlic	5 ml
2 (15 ounce) cans Italian stewed tomatoes	2 (425 g)
1 teaspoon Italian seasoning	5 ml
8 ounces rotini pasta, cooked al dente, drained	227 g
1 (8 ounce) package shredded mozzarella cheese, divided	227 g
1 (2 ounce) can pitted ripe olives, halved	57 g

• Cook Italian sausage in large skillet until slices are no longer pink, about 10 minutes. Remove sausage from skillet and save about 2 tablespoons (30 ml) drippings.

• Saute mushrooms, onions, bell pepper and garlic in skillet just until tender-crisp.

• In large bowl, combine sausage, mushroom-bell pepper mixture, stewed tomatoes, Italian seasoning, pasta and half of mozzarella cheese and mix well.

• Spoon into greased 3-quart (3 L) baking dish. Cover and bake at 350° (176°C) for 30 minutes.

• Remove from oven, sprinkle remaining cheese over top of casserole and return to oven for 5 minutes.

• When ready to serve, sprinkle olives over top of casserole.

A Special Rice

3/4 cup pine nuts	180 ml
3 tablespoons orange juice	45 ml
1 cup dried currants	240 ml
1 cup brown rice	240 ml
1 cup white rice	240 ml
2 tablespoons grated orange zest	30 ml
2 tablespoons snipped parsley	30 ml
4 tablespoons olive oil	60 ml
1 (3 ounce) package grated parmesan cheese	84 g

• Spread out pine nuts over baking sheet and bake at 250° (121° C) for 10 to 15 minutes and stir once. Remove from oven and set aside.

• Pour orange juice over currants and set aside.

• Cook brown rice and white rice according to package directions and mix in separate bowl.

• Add pine nuts, currants, orange zest, parsley, olive oil, ½ teaspoon (2 ml) each of salt and pepper to rice mixture. Mix thoroughly.

• Spoon mixture into sprayed baking dish, cover with foil and bake at 350° (176° C) for 15 to 20 minutes until hot.

• Sprinkle parmesan cheese over top.

Festive Cranberries

What a great dish for Thanksgiving or Christmas!

2 (20 ounce) cans pie apples*	2 (567 g)
1 (16 ounce) can whole cranberries	.5 kg
¾ cup sugar	180 ml
½ cup packed brown sugar	120 ml

Topping:

¼ cup (½ stick) butter	60 ml
1½ cups crushed corn flakes	360 ml
⅔ cup sugar	160 ml
½ teaspoon ground cinnamon	2 ml
1 cup chopped pecans	240 ml

- Combine pie apples, cranberries and both sugars in bowl and mix well. Spoon into buttered 2-quart (2 L) baking dish.

- Melt butter in saucepan and mix in corn flakes, sugar, cinnamon and pecans.

- Sprinkle over apples and cranberries.

- Bake uncovered at 325° (162° C) for 1 hour. This can be served hot or at room temperature.

*Tip: Look for pie apples, not apple pie filling.

Early Morning Vegetable Lasagna

This is "early morning" because it's so easy you can make it in the morning, go to work or play and it's ready to pop in the oven whenever you are ready. While it's cookin', you can be chillin'!

1 (14 ounce) can Italian-style stewed tomatoes 396 g
1½ cups pasta sauce 360 ml
2 cups cottage cheese, drained 480 ml
1 cup grated parmesan cheese 240 ml
9 lasagna noodles, uncooked, divided
4 zucchini, shredded, divided
7 (1 ounce) provolone cheese slices,
cut into strips, divided 7 (28 g)

- Stir stewed tomatoes and pasta sauce and set aside.

- Stir cottage cheese, parmesan cheese, ¼ teaspoon (1 ml) each of salt and pepper.

- Spoon one-third tomato mixture into sprayed 9 x 13-inch (23 x 33 cm) baking dish.

- Place 3 uncooked lasagna noodles over tomato mixture and top with one-third grated zucchini.

- Spoon one-third cheese mixture over zucchini and top with one-third provolone cheese strips.

- Repeat layering procedure twice. Cover and chill at least 8 hours.

- Remove from refrigerator and let stand for 30 minutes. Bake covered at 350° (176° C) for 45 minutes.

- Uncover and bake additional 20 minutes. Let stand 15 minutes before serving.

Vegetables

Sunshine On the Table

This is absolutely the prettiest casserole you will place on your table! And not only pretty, but it is also tasty, delicious, delectable, savory, appetizing, classic and elegant. Need I go on? You'll never want a simple, buttered carrot again!

2½ cups carrots, finely shredded	600 ml	
2 cups cooked rice	480 ml	
2 eggs, beaten		
2 cups cubed processed cheese	480 ml	
1 (15 ounce) can cream-style corn	425 g	
¼ cup half-and-half cream	60 ml	
2 tablespoons (¼ stick) butter, melted	30 ml	
2 tablespoons dried minced onion	30 ml	

• Combine all ingredients and ½ teaspoon (2 ml) each of salt and pepper in large bowl.

• Spoon into buttered 3-quart (3 L) baking dish.

• Bake uncovered at 350° (176° C) for 40 minutes or until set.

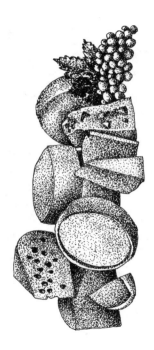

Cheddar-Broccoli Bake

1 (10 ounce) can cheddar cheese soup	280 g
1 (8 ounce) package cheddar-jack cheese	227 g
⅓ cup milk	80 ml
1 cup celery, chopped	240 ml
1 sweet red bell pepper, julienned	
1 (16 ounce) bag frozen broccoli florets,	
cooked	.5 kg
1 (6 ounce) can french-fried onion rings	168 g

• Combine soup, cheese, milk, celery, bell pepper, broccoli and ½ teaspoon (2 ml) each of salt and pepper in bowl and mix well.

• Pour into buttered 3-quart (3 L) baking dish. Cover and bake at 325° (162° C) for 25 minutes.

• Uncover, sprinkle onion rings over casserole and return to oven for 15 minutes or until onion rings are golden brown.

Broccoli Supreme

2 (10 ounce) packages broccoli spears	2 (280 g)
1 stick garlic cheese roll	
1 (10 ounce) can cream of mushroom soup	280 g
1 (3 ounce) can sliced mushrooms, drained	84 g
¾ cup seasoned breadcrumbs	180 ml

- Boil broccoli for 3 minutes in saucepan and drain. Place broccoli in 2-quart (2 L) baking dish.

- In another saucepan, combine cheese roll, soup and mushrooms. Heat on medium, stirring constantly, until cheese melts.

- Spoon cheese-mushroom mixture over broccoli. Sprinkle breadcrumbs over top of casserole.

- Bake uncovered at 350° (176° C) for 30 minutes.

Broccoli is such a wonderful vegetable, so green, pretty and healthy too! There are so many ways to serve it, plain buttered, loaded with cheeses, baked in soufflé, creamed and crunchy good raw. It really perks up salad and makes it special.

Impossible Broccoli Pie

1 (16 ounce) package frozen broccoli spears,
  thawed .5 kg
1 (12 ounce) package shredded cheddar cheese,
  divided 340 g
½ cup onion, chopped 120 ml
3 eggs, slightly beaten
¾ cup buttermilk biscuit mix 180 ml
1½ cups milk 360 ml

- Cut broccoli into smaller pieces and discard some stems.

- In large mixing bowl, combine broccoli, two-thirds of cheese and all onion and mix well. Spoon into greased 10-inch (25 cm), deep-dish, pie plate.

- Mix eggs and biscuit mix in same mixing bowl and beat for several minutes.

- Add milk and ¾ teaspoon (4 ml) each of salt and pepper and mix until fairly smooth. Pour over broccoli and cheese mixture.

- Bake uncovered at 350° (176° C) for 35 to 40 minutes or until knife inserted in center comes out clean.

- Top with remaining cheese and bake just until cheese melts. Let stand 5 minute before slicing to serve.

Broccoli Souffle

4 cups fresh broccoli florets	1 L	
5 tablespoons butter, melted	75 ml	
2 tablespoons flour	30 ml	
3 eggs, beaten		
1 cup small curd cottage cheese, drained	240 ml	
½ cup half-and-half cream	120 ml	
1 cup shredded cheddar cheese, divided	240 ml	
½ cup minced onion	120 ml	

- Cut broccoli into very small florets with very little stem. Place florets and 2 tablespoons (30 ml) water in microwave-safe bowl. Microwave on HIGH for 3 minutes.

- Remove from microwave, add butter, sprinkle flour over broccoli and toss.

- In bowl with beaten eggs, add cottage cheese, cream, ½ cup (120 ml) cheese, onion, ½ teaspoon (2 ml) each salt and pepper and mix well.

- Combine broccoli and egg mixture and pour into buttered 7 x 11-inch (18 x 28 cm) baking dish or souffle dish. Sprinkle remaining ½ cup (120 ml) cheese over top.

- Bake uncovered at 350° (176° C) for 30 to 35 minutes or until center sets.

Broccoli Frittata

3 tablespoons butter	45 ml
½ cup onion, chopped	120 ml
4 cups fresh broccoli florets, without stems	1 L
6 large eggs	
1 (1 ounce) envelope cream of broccoli soup mix	28 g
½ cup shredded cheddar cheese	120 ml
½ cup milk	120 ml

- Melt butter in skillet and saute onion. Add broccoli and 1 tablespoon (15 ml) water. Cook, stirring occasionally, on low heat for about 5 minutes until just tender crisp, but still bright green.

- Whisk eggs, soup mix, cheese, milk, and ½ teaspoon (2 ml) each of salt and pepper in separate bowl. Fold in broccoli-onion mixture.

- Pour into buttered 10-inch (25 cm), deep-dish pie pan.

- Bake at 350° (176° C) for 20 to 25 minutes or until center sets.

- Let frittata cool for 5 or 10 minutes before cutting into wedges to serve.

Vegetables

Broccoli-Rice Whiz

So easy and so good! And it gives us a vegetable and rice all in one dish.

2 cups instant rice	480 ml
3/4 cup onion, chopped	180 ml
3/4 cup sweet red bell pepper, chopped	180 ml
3/4 cup celery, chopped	180 ml
1/4 cup (1/2 stick) butter	60 ml
1 (8 ounce) jar Mexican processed cheese spread	227 g
1 (10 ounce) can cream of chicken soup	280 g
1/2 cup whole milk	120 ml
2 (10 ounce) packages frozen chopped broccoli, thawed, drained	2 (280 g)

- Cook rice in large saucepan.

- Saute onions, bell pepper and celery in butter.

- Add onion-celery mixture to rice. Fold in cheese, chicken soup and milk and mix well.

- Heat on low until cheese and soup blends well. Fold in chopped broccoli.

- Pour into large greased 3-quart (3 L) baking dish and bake covered at 350° (176° C) for 35 minutes.

Broccoli-Cauliflower Casserole

1 (10 ounce) box frozen broccoli florets, thawed	280 g
1 (10 ounce) box frozen cauliflower, thawed	280 g
1 egg, beaten	
⅔ cup mayonnaise	160 ml
1 (10 ounce) can cream of chicken soup	280 g
¼ cup whole milk	60 ml
1 onion, chopped	
1 sweet red bell pepper, seeded, chopped	
1 cup grated Swiss cheese	240 ml
1 cup seasoned breadcrumbs	240 ml
2 tablespoons (¼ stick) butter	30 ml

• Cook broccoli and cauliflower according to package directions. Drain well and place in large mixing bowl.

• In saucepan, combine egg, mayonnaise, soup, milk, onion, bell pepper and cheese and mix well. Heat just enough to be able to mix well.

• Spoon into mixing bowl with broccoli-cauliflower and mix well. Pour into a 2½-quart (2.5 L) buttered baking dish.

• Combine breadcrumbs and butter and sprinkle over broccoli and cauliflower mixture.

• Bake uncovered at 350° (176° C) for 35 minutes.

Cauliflower Melody

1 head cauliflower, cut into florets	
1 (15 ounce) can Italian stewed tomatoes, with juice	425 g
1 onion, finely chopped	
1 green bell pepper, sliced	
1 tablespoon sugar	15 ml
1 tablespoon cornstarch	15 ml
¼ cup (½ stick) butter, melted	60 ml
1 cup shredded cheddar cheese	240 ml
1 cup Italian seasoned breadcrumbs	240 ml

• Cook cauliflower in large saucepan with salted water for about 10 minutes or until tender-crisp and drain well.

• Combine stewed tomatoes, onion, bell pepper, sugar, cornstarch, melted butter and ½ teaspoon (2 ml) each of salt and pepper and mix well.

• Transfer cauliflower and tomato mixture to 2-quart (2 L) baking dish and sprinkle cheese, and breadcrumbs over top.

• Bake uncovered at 350° (176° C) for 35 minutes.

Baked Cauliflower

1 (16 ounce) package frozen cauliflower, thawed	.5 kg
1 egg	
⅔ cup mayonnaise	160 ml
1 (10 ounce) can cream of chicken soup	280 g
4 ounces Swiss cheese, grated	114 g
2 ribs celery, sliced	
1 green bell pepper, chopped	
1 onion, chopped	
1½ cups round buttery cracker crumbs	360 ml

• Butter 9 x 13-inch (23 x 33 cm) baking dish. Place cauliflower in dish and cover loosely with plastic wrap.

• Cook on HIGH in microwave for 3 minutes. Turn dish and cook another 3 minutes.

• In medium saucepan, combine egg, mayonnaise, chicken soup and grated cheese. Heat just until ingredients mix.

• Add celery, bell pepper, onion and 1 teaspoon (5 ml) pepper to cauliflower and mix well. Pour soup mixture over vegetables and spread out.

• Sprinkle cracker crumbs on top.

• Bake uncovered at 350° (176° C) for 35 to 40 minutes or until crumbs are light brown.

Cauliflower Con Queso

1 large head cauliflower, broken into florets	
¼ cup (½ stick) butter	60 ml
½ onion, chopped	
2 tablespoons flour	30 ml
1 (15 ounce) can Mexican-stewed tomatoes	425 g
1 (4 ounce) can chopped green chilies, drained	114 g
1½ cups shredded Monterey Jack cheese	360 ml

- Cook cauliflower florets until just tender-crisp, drain and place in buttered 2-quart (2 L) baking dish.

- Melt butter in medium saucepan. Saute onion just until clear, but not brown.

- Blend in flour and stir in tomatoes. Cook, stirring constantly, until mixture thickens.

- Add green chilies and ¾ teaspoon (4 ml) each of salt and pepper.

- Fold in cheese and stir until it melts. Pour sauce over drained cauliflower.

- Cover and bake at 325° (162° C) for about 15 minutes.

Cauliflower may be cooked and buttered, dressed up with creamy white sauce, cheeses or perked up with Italian tomatoes. "Raw" will add flavor and crunch to any green salad. Cauliflower is a member of the cabbage family, but it beats cabbage by a mile Mark Twain said "cauliflower is nothing but cabbage with a college education." Education is good!

Cheese to the Rescue

1 large head cauliflower, cut into florets	
1 sweet red bell pepper, sliced	
½ cup celery, chopped	120 ml
½ cup (1 stick) butter, divided	120 ml
1 (10 ounce) box frozen green peas, thawed	280 g
1 (8 ounce) package shredded Mexican 4-cheese blend, divided	227 g
⅓ cup flour	80 ml
1 pint half-and-half cream	.5 kg
½ cup milk	120 ml

• Cook cauliflower, in covered saucepan with small amount of water until tender-crisp. Don't overcook.

• Saute bell pepper and celery in small skillet in 3 tablespoons (45 ml) butter.

• Add bell pepper, celery and peas to drained cauliflower and toss with half the cheese.

• Spoon into buttered 3-quart (3 L) baking dish.

• Combine remaining butter, flour, and ½ teaspoon (2 ml) each of salt and pepper in another saucepan and mix well.

• On medium high heat gradually add cream and milk. Cook, stirring constantly, until mixture thickens. Pour over vegetables. Cove and bake at 325° (162° C) for 20 minutes.

• Uncover and sprinkle remaining cheese over top of casserole. Return to oven for 5 minutes.

Crunchy Cauliflower and Friends

1 large head cauliflower, broken into florets		
1 zucchini, cut in large pieces		
1 sweet red bell pepper, sliced		
1 (8 ounce) can whole kernel corn, drained	227 g	
1 (8 ounce) carton sour cream	227 g	
1 cup grated cheddar cheese	240 ml	
½ cup crushed corn flakes	120 ml	
¾ cup buttery cracker crumbs, crushed	180 ml	
⅓ cup grated parmesan cheese	80 ml	

- Combine cauliflower, zucchini and bell pepper in large saucepan, cover and cook in small amount of water for 5 to 7 minutes and drain.

- Combine cauliflower-zucchini mixture, corn, 1 teaspoon (5 ml) each of salt and pepper, sour cream and cheddar cheese and mix just until sour cream and cheddar cheese coats vegetables.

- Combine corn flakes and cracker crumbs.

- Sprinkle crumb mixture over vegetables and mix lightly.

- Spoon vegetables into greased 9 x 13-inch (23 x 33 cm) baking dish. Sprinkle parmesan cheese over top of casserole.

- Bake uncovered at 325° (162° C) for about 30 minutes or until crumbs are light brown.

Grand Cauliflower

¾ cup cooked, finely chopped ham	180 ml
2 cloves garlic, finely minced	
1 sweet red bell pepper, chopped	
½ cup onion, chopped	120 ml
6 tablespoons (¾ stick) butter, divided	90 ml
1 (16 ounce) package frozen cauliflower, thawed	.5 kg
2 tablespoons flour	30 ml
1½ cups whipping cream	360 ml
1½ cups shredded cheddar cheese	360 ml
½ cup almond slivers, toasted	120 ml
3 tablespoons minced fresh parsley	45 ml

• Saute ham, garlic, red bell pepper and onion in large skillet over medium heat, in 2 tablespoons (30 ml) butter. Add cauliflower and 2 tablespoons (30 ml) water, cover and steam until tender-crisp.

• Melt remaining butter in separate skillet. Add flour, a little salt and pepper and a little bit cream and stir well to blend.

• Add remaining cream, heat and cook, stirring constantly, until mixture thickens. Add cheese and stir.

• Spoon cauliflower-ham mixture into greased 2-quart (2 L) baking dish. Pour cream mixture over cauliflower. Sprinkle almonds on top of casserole.

• Cover and bake at 350° (176° C) for 20 minutes, just until casserole is hot.

Spinach Enchiladas

Wow, are these good and this recipe freezes well.

2 (10 ounce) boxes chopped spinach, thawed, pressed dry	2 (280 g)
1 (1 ounce) envelope dry onion soup mix	28 g
3 cups shredded cheddar cheese, divided	710 ml
3 cups shredded Monterey Jack cheese or mozzarella, divided	710 ml
12 flour tortillas	
1 pint whipping cream	.5 kg

• Use lots of paper towels to make sure spinach is well drained.

• Combine spinach and onion soup mix in medium bowl. Blend in 1½ cups (360 ml) cheddar and 1½ cups (360 ml) jack cheeses.

• Spread out 12 tortillas and place about 3 heaping tablespoons (45 ml) spinach mixture down middle of each tortilla and roll.

• Place each filled tortilla, seam-side down, into greased 10 x 14-inch (25 x 36 cm) baking dish.

• Pour whipping cream over enchiladas and sprinkle with remaining cheeses.

• Cover and bake at 350° (176° C) for 20 minutes.

• Uncover and bake another 10 minutes longer.

Tip: To make ahead of time, freeze before adding whipping cream and remaining cheeses. Thaw in refrigerator before cooking. These enchiladas are great and so much fun to make and serve! Eat them all up because the tortillas get a little tough if reheated.

Spinach Delight

This great casserole may be made in advance and baked when ready to serve.

2 (10 ounce) boxes frozen, chopped spinach, thawed	2 (280 g)
1 (16 ounce) carton small curd cottage cheese	.5 kg
3 cups grated white cheddar cheese	710 ml
4 eggs, beaten	
3 tablespoons flour	45 ml
¼ cup (½ stick) butter, melted	60 ml
½ teaspoon garlic salt	2 ml
½ teaspoon celery salt	2 ml
½ teaspoon lemon pepper	2 ml
1 tablespoon dried onion flakes	15 ml

• Drain spinach well by squeezing with several paper towels.

• Mix spinach, cottage cheese, cheddar cheese, eggs, flour, butter, seasonings and onion flakes in large bowl.

• Pour into buttered 2½ -quart (2.5 L) baking dish.

• Bake at 325° (162° C) for 1 hour.

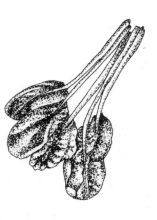

Spinach Special

Eat something green on New Year's Day to have money in the New Year. It's a great tradition and this is the dish to go with the tradition.

3 (10 ounce) packages frozen chopped spinach 3 (280 g)
1 onion, chopped
½ cup (1 stick) butter   120 ml
1 (8 ounce) package cream cheese, cubed   227 g
1 (14 ounce) can artichokes, drained, chopped 396 g
⅔ cup grated parmesan cheese   160 ml

• Cook spinach according to package directions in saucepan. Drain thoroughly and set aside.

• In skillet saute onion in butter, stir and cook until onion is clear but not brown.

• On low heat add cream cheese and stir constantly until cheese melts.

• Stir in spinach, artichokes and ½ teaspoon (2 ml) each of salt and pepper.

• Pour into greased 2-quart (2 L) baking dish. Sprinkle parmesan cheese over top of casserole.

• Cover and bake at 350° (176° C) for 30 minutes.

Easy Creamy Spinach

2 (10 ounce) packages frozen chopped spinach	2 (280 g)	
1 (8 ounce) package cream cheese and chives, softened	227 g	
⅔ cup shredded cheddar cheese	160 ml	
1 (10 ounce) can cream of celery soup	280 g	
½ cup milk	120 ml	
1 egg, beaten		
1 cup cheese cracker crumbs	240 ml	

• Cook spinach in saucepan according to package directions and drain well.

• Add cream cheese and cheddar cheese to hot spinach, stir until both cheeses melt and mix well.

• Stir in soup, milk and egg and mix well.

• Pour into 2-quart (2 L) buttered baking dish. Top with cheese cracker crumbs.

• Bake uncovered for 350° (176° C) for about 35 minutes.

Confetti-Squash Casserole

What a great vegetable dish and it is a very attractive dish as well!

1 pound yellow squash, sliced	.5 kg	
1 pound zucchini, sliced	.5 kg	
1 large onion, chopped		
¾ cup green bell pepper, chopped	180 ml	
1 (10 ounce) can cream of chicken soup	280 g	
1 (8 ounce) carton sour cream	227 g	
1 (4 ounce) jar chopped pimento, drained	114 g	
1 (8 ounce) can sliced water chestnuts, drained	227 g	
2 small carrots, grated		
½ cup (1 stick) butter	120 ml	
1 (6 ounce) box herb stuffing mix	168 g	

- Cook squash, zucchini, onion and bell pepper in salted water for barely 10 minutes or until just tender-crisp and drain well. (Be sure not to overcook).

- In separate bowl, combine chicken soup, sour cream, pimento, water chestnuts and carrots and mix well.

- Melt butter in large saucepan and add stuffing mix with its seasoning packet.

- Add squash-bell pepper mixture and soup-carrots mixture and mix gently, but well.

- Spoon into buttered 3-quart (3 L) baking dish.

- Bake uncovered at 325° (162° C) for 35 minutes.

Yummy Yellow Squash

4 cups squash, sliced	1 L
1 onion, chopped	
1 carrot, finely grated	
1 (3 ounce) package cream cheese, softened, cubed	84 g
1 (4 ounce) jar chopped pimento, drained	114 g
1 (8 ounce) carton sour cream	227 g
1 cup small curd cottage cheese, drained	240 ml
1½ cup Monterey Jack cheese	360 ml
6 tablespoons (¾ stick) butter, melted, divided	90 ml
1 (6 ounce) package chicken-flavor stuffing mix, divided	168 g

- Cook squash, onion and grated carrot with a little salted water in large saucepan until tender-crisp. Drain.

- While mixture is still hot, fold in cream cheese and stir until it melts.

- Add pimento, sour cream, cottage cheese, Monterey Jack cheese and about 4 tablespoons (60 ml) melted butter and mix well.

- Stir in half stuffing mix and all of seasoning package included with mix and fold into squash mixture. Spoon into lightly greased 3-quart (3 L) baking dish.

- Sprinkle remaining stuffing over top and drizzle remaining melted butter over top.

- Bake uncovered at 350° (176° C) for 35 minutes.

Posh Squash

3 pounds yellow squash, sliced	1.3 kg	
1 onion, chopped		
1 (8 ounce) package grated processed cheese	227 g	
2 eggs, beaten		
1 tablespoon sugar	15 ml	
1 (4 ounce) jar chopped pimentos	114 g	
6 tablespoons (¾ stick) plus	90 ml	
4 tablespoons butter, melted	60 ml	
2 cups cracker crumbs	480 ml	
1 (3 ounce) can fried onion rings	84 g	

- Boil squash and onion in large saucepan until tender. Drain and mash with potato masher.

- Add cheese, stirring constantly and heat on low burner just until cheese melts. Add eggs, sugar, pimentos and 6 tablespoons (90 ml) butter and blend well.

- Pour into buttered 9 x 13-inch (23 x 33 cm) baking dish.

- Mix crumbs and 4 tablespoons (60 ml) butter and sprinkle over casserole.

- Bake uncovered at 350° (176° C) for 35 minutes.

- Add fried onion rings to top and bake additional 10 minutes.

Zucchini Bake

3 cups zucchini, grated	710 ml
1½ cups grated Monterey Jack cheese	360 ml
4 eggs, beaten	
¼ teaspoon garlic powder	1 ml
2 cups cheese cracker crumbs	480 ml

- Combine zucchini, cheese, eggs, garlic powder and ½ teaspoon (2 ml) each of salt and pepper and mix well. Spoon into buttered 2-quart (2 L) baking dish.

- Sprinkle cracker crumbs over top.

- Bake uncovered at 350° (176° C) for 35 to 40 minutes.

Zucchini is a popular summer squash that has a light and delicate flavor. When buying zucchini, select the smaller ones which will have a thinner skin. This delicious vegetable can be cooked many different ways or eaten raw in salads. Try adding sliced or chopped raw zucchini to your next green salad. You'll love the addition.

Zippy Zucchini

4 eggs	
1 (8 ounce) package shredded Monterey Jack cheese	227 g
4 cups zucchini, grated	1 L
1 (4 ounce) cup green chilies, chopped	114 g
1 (4 ounce) jar sliced pimentos, drained	114 g
1 onion, finely minced	
1 teaspoon Creole seasoning	5 ml
1½ cups seasoned croutons, crushed	360 ml
1 (3 ounce) package grated parmesan cheese	84 g

- Beat eggs well in large mixing bowl. Stir in cheese, zucchini, green chilies, pimentos, onion, Creole seasoning and ½ teaspoon (2 ml) pepper and mix well.

- Pour into well greased 2-quart (2 L) baking dish.

- Bake uncovered at 350° (176° C) for 35 minutes.

- Mix crushed croutons and parmesan cheese and set aside.

- After 35 minutes of baking, sprinkle crouton mixture over casserole and bake another 10 minutes.

Zucchini-on-the-Ritz

3 pounds zucchini, sliced	1.3 kg
1 sweet red bell pepper, finely diced	
6 tablespoons (¾ stick) butter	90 ml
2 tablespoons flour	30 ml
1 (5 ounce) can evaporated milk	143 g
¼ cup milk	60 ml
1 (8 ounce) package grated processed cheese	227 g
1 (4 ounce) can chopped green chilies	114 g
1 (4 ounce) jar chopped pimentos	114 g
2½ cups butter crackers, crushed	600 ml
⅓ cup slivered almonds	80 ml

• Boil zucchini and bell pepper in saucepan just until barely tender, but do not overcook.

• Melt butter in large saucepan, stir in flour and mix well. Slowly add both milks and cook, stirring constantly on low heat, until white sauce is thick and smooth.

• Stir in cheese and heat just until cheese melts.

• Add chilies, pimentos, a little salt and pepper and fold in cooked, well-drained zucchini-bell pepper mixture.

• Pour into greased 3-quart (3 L) baking dish and top with cracker crumbs.

• Sprinkle almonds over top of crumbs.

• Bake uncovered at 325° (162° C) for 35 minutes or until hot and bubbly.

Tip: This delicious zucchini dish may be made the day before, but wait to add crumbs and almonds until you cook it.

Not-Your-Banquet Beans

You didn't really want plain green beans, did you?

3 (15 ounce) cut green beans, drained	3 (425 g)	
1 (8 ounce) can sliced water chestnuts, drained, chopped	227 g	
½ cup slivered almonds	120 ml	
½ cup roasted sweet red bell peppers, chopped	120 ml	
1 (16 ounce) package cubed Mexican processed cheese	.5 kg	
1½ cups cracker crumbs	360 ml	
¼ cup (½ stick) butter, melted	60 ml	

• Place green beans in buttered 9 x 13-inch (23 x 33 cm) baking dish and cover with water chestnuts, almonds and roasted, red bell pepper.

• Spread cheese over green bean-almond mixture.

• Place casserole in microwave and heat just barely enough for cheese to begin to melt. (Watch closely).

• Combine cracker crumbs and butter and sprinkle over casserole.

• Bake uncovered at 350° (176° C) for 30 minutes.

Fancy Green Bean Bake

2 (16 ounce) packages frozen French-style green beans, thawed	2 (.5 kg)
½ cup (1 stick) butter	120 ml
1 (8 ounce) package fresh mushrooms, sliced	227 g
1 onion, chopped	
¼ cup flour	60 ml
1 pint half-and-half cream	.5 kg
1 cup milk	240 ml
½ cup roasted red bell peppers, chopped	120 ml
2 teaspoons soy sauce	10 ml
1 cup shredded cheddar cheese	240 ml
⅔ cup chopped cashew nuts	160 ml
½ cup chow mein noodles	120 ml

• Cook green beans according to package directions, drain and set aside.

• In large saucepan, melt butter and saute mushrooms and chopped onion. Stir in flour and cook on medium heat for 1 minute, stirring constantly.

• Gradually add cream and milk and stir until they blend.

• Add red peppers, soy sauce, cheese and ½ teaspoon (2 ml) each of salt and pepper. Stir constantly until cheese melts and mixture is thick.

• Combine sauce and green beans and pour into greased 9 x 13-inch (23 x 33 cm) baking dish.

• Combine cashews and chow mein noodles and sprinkle over top of casserole.

• Bake uncovered at 325° (162° C) for 30 minutes.

Green Bean Supreme

2 tablespoons (¼ stick) butter   30 ml
1 (10 ounce) can cream of mushroom soup   280 g
1 (3 ounce) package cream cheese, softened   84 g
3 (15 ounce) cans French-style green beans, drained   3 (425 g)
1 tablespoon dried onion flakes   15 ml
1 (8 ounce) can sliced water chestnuts, drained
½ teaspoon garlic powder   2 ml
1½ cups shredded cheddar cheese   360 ml
1½ cups cracker crumbs   360 ml
½ cup slivered almonds   120 ml

- Melt butter in large saucepan and add soup and cream cheese. Cook over low heat, stirring constantly, just until cream cheese melts and mixture is fairly smooth.

- Remove from heat and stir in green beans, onion flakes, water chestnuts, garlic powder, cheese and ½ teaspoon (2 ml) salt. Mix well.

- Pour into buttered 9 x 13-inch (23 x 33 cm) baking dish. Top with cracker crumbs and sprinkle with almonds.

- Bake uncovered at 350° (176° C) for 30 minutes or until casserole bubbles around edges.

Bundles of Green

3 (15 ounce) cans whole green beans, drained   3 (425 g)
1 pound bacon   .5 kg
2 (15 ounce) cans new potatoes, drained   2 (425 g)
2 (10 ounce) cans fiesta nacho cheese soup   2 (280 g)
1½ cups milk   360 ml

• Place 6 to 7 whole green beans in bundle; wrap with ½ strip of bacon and secure with toothpicks.

• Place bundles in large baking dish so bundles do not touch. Place under broiler in oven until bacon cooks on both sides.

• Spoon off bacon drippings and place potatoes around bundles.

• In saucepan combine nacho cheese soup and milk and heat just enough to mix well. Pour over green beans and potatoes.

• Cover and bake at 350° (176° C) for 20 minutes or just until sauce bubbles.

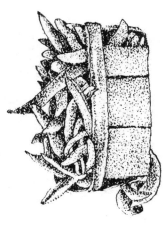

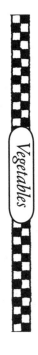

Green Bean Delight

Deluxe Green Beans

2 (15 ounce) cans French-style green beans,
   drained   2 (425 g)
1 (10 ounce) can cream of chicken soup   280 g
1 (15 ounce) can shoe-peg corn, drained   425 g
1 onion, chopped
1 sweet red bell pepper, chopped
1 cup celery, finely chopped   240 ml
1 (8 ounce) can sliced water chestnuts,
   drained
1 (8 ounce) carton sour cream   227 g
1 cup grated processed cheese   227 g
3 tablespoons butter   240 ml
1 cup butter-flavored crackers, crushed   45 ml
⅓ cup slivered almonds   240 ml
   80 ml

- Combine green beans, soup, corn, onion, bell pepper, celery, water chestnuts, sour cream and cheese in large bowl and mix well. Transfer to greased 9 x 13-inch (23 x 33 cm) baking dish.

- In skillet, melt butter, and add cracker crumbs and almonds. Cook over low heat and stir until light brown. Sprinkle over top of casserole.

- Bake uncovered at 350° (176° C) for 45 minutes or until topping is golden brown.

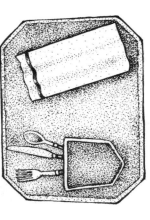

Beans and More Beans

½ pound bacon	227 g	
2 large onions, chopped		
1 cup celery, chopped	240 ml	
1 cup green bell pepper, chopped	240 ml	
1½ cups packed brown sugar	360 ml	
⅓ cup cider vinegar	80 ml	
1 tablespoon prepared mustard	15 ml	
1 (15 ounce) can kidney beans, rinsed, drained	425 g	
1 (15 ounce) can navy beans, rinsed, drained	425 g	
1 (15 ounce) can lima beans, rinsed, drained	425 g	
1 (15 ounce) can pork and beans, with liquid	425 g	
1 (15 ounce) can pinto beans, drained	425 g	

- Cook bacon in large skillet until crisp and drain.

- With bacon drippings remaining in skillet, saute onions, celery and bell pepper. Add brown sugar, vinegar, mustard and 1 teaspoon (5 ml) salt.

- Combine onion, bell pepper, bacon and all beans in large bowl. Pour into buttered 4-quart (4 L) baking dish.

- Cover and bake at 325° (162° C) for 2 hours.

Country Baked Beans

4 (15 ounce) cans baked beans, drained   4 (425 g)
1 (8 ounce) bottle chili sauce   227 g
1 onion, chopped
½ pound bacon, cooked, crumbled   227 g
2 cups packed brown sugar   480 ml

• Combine all ingredients in ungreased 3-quart (3 L)
baking dish. Stir until they blend well.

• Bake uncovered at 325° (162° C) for 55 minutes or
until bubbly around edges.

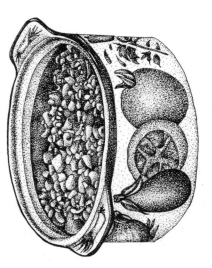

Corn-Zucchini Success

3 zucchini, with peel	
½ cup green bell peppers, chopped	120 ml
½ cup red bell pepper, chopped	120 ml
½ cup onion, chopped	120 ml
5 tablespoons butter, divided	75 ml
¼ cup flour	60 ml
1 (15 ounce) can cream-style corn	425 g
1 (3 ounce) package cream cheese, cubed	84 g
⅔ cup grated Swiss cheese	160 ml
1 (15 ounce) can whole kernel corn, drained	425 g
½ cup chopped pecans	120 ml
1 cup seasoned breadcrumbs	240 ml

- Grate zucchini, drain well on paper towels and set aside.

- Saute bell peppers and onion in 2 tablespoons (30 ml) butter in saucepan. Add remaining butter, flour and ½ teaspoon (2 ml) each of salt and pepper and mix well.

- On medium-high heat, add cream-style corn, stirring constantly, until mixture thickens.

- Add pepper-onion mixture, cream cheese and Swiss cheese and heat on low until cheeses melt.

- Add whole kernel corn, zucchini and pecans and mix well. Spoon into butter 2-quart (2 L) baking dish.

- Sprinkle breadcrumbs over top of casserole.

- Bake uncovered at 350° (176° C) for 30 minutes or until breadcrumbs are light brown.

Corn With An Attitude

1 (15 ounce) can whole kernel corn	425 g
1 (15 ounce) can cream-style corn	425 g
½ cup (1 stick) butter, melted	120 ml
2 eggs, beaten	
1 (8 ounce) carton sour cream	227 g
1 (6 ounce) package jalapeno cornbread mix	168 g
½ cup shredded cheddar cheese	120 ml

• Mix all ingredients, except cheese in large bowl.

• Pour into buttered 9 x 13-inch (23 x 33 cm) baking dish.

• Bake uncovered at 350° (176° C) for 35 minutes.

• Uncover and sprinkle cheese on top of casserole. Return to oven for 5 minutes.

Tip: You will probably find this corn casserole or a very similar version at church suppers. And the dish will always be empty at the end of the evening.

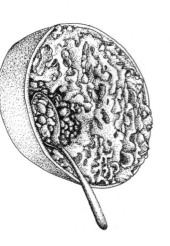

Kid-Pleasing Corn

3 eggs, beaten	
1 (8 ounce) carton sour cream	227 g
½ cup yellow cornmeal	120 ml
½ cup (1 stick) butter, melted	120 ml
1 (8 ounce) can cream-style corn	227 g
1 (15 ounce) can whole kernel yellow corn, drained	425 g
1 (8 ounce) package shredded cheddar-jack cheese	227 g
½ teaspoon celery salt	2 ml

- In bowl, combine all ingredients, 1 teaspoon (5 ml) salt and ¼ teaspoon (1 ml) pepper and mix well. Pour into greased 2-quart (2 L) baking dish.

- Bake uncovered at 350° (176° C) for 45 minutes or until center sets. Let stand 5 minutes before serving.

Fiesta Corn

1 (15 ounce) can cream-style corn	425 g
1 (15 ounce) can whole kernel corn, drained	425 g
1 bell pepper, seeded, chopped	
1 onion, chopped	
1 (4 ounce) can chopped green chilies	114 g
2 tablespoons (¼ stick) butter, melted	30 ml
2 eggs beaten	
1 tablespoon sugar	15 ml
1½ cups buttery cracker crumbs, divided	360 ml
1 cup shredded 4-cheese blend	240 ml
1 cup butter-cracker crumbs	240 ml
2 tablespoons grated parmesan cheese	30 ml

• Mix both cans of corn, bell pepper, onion, green chilies, butter, eggs, sugar, ½ cup (120 ml) cracker crumbs, cheese and some salt, pepper and cayenne, if on hand.

• Pour into buttered 9 x 13-inch (23 x 33 cm) baking dish.

• Combine remaining 1 cup (240 ml) cracker crumbs and parmesan cheese and sprinkle over casserole.

• Bake uncovered at 350° (176° C) for 45 minutes.

Scalloped Corn and Tomatoes

2 (15 ounce) cans Mexican-stewed tomatoes,
   with juice   2 (425 g)
2 (15 ounce) cans whole kernel corn, drained   2 (425 g)
½ cup (1 stick) butter, melted, divided   120 ml
1 (8 ounce) package shredded cheddar cheese   227 g
1 onion, chopped
2 tablespoons cornstarch   30 ml
2 eggs, beaten
2 teaspoons sugar   10 ml
½ teaspoon garlic powder   2 ml
1½ cups round buttery cracker crumbs   360 ml

- Mix tomatoes, corn, 6 tablespoons (90 ml) butter, cheese, onion, cornstarch, eggs, sugar and 1 teaspoon (5 ml) each of salt and pepper. Pour into buttered 9 x 13-inch (23 x 33 cm) baking dish.

- Bake uncovered at 350° (176° C) for 35 minutes.

- In small bowl, mix crumbs and 2 tablespoons (30 ml) butter. Sprinkle over top of casserole.

- Bake uncovered for 15 minutes more.

Asparagus Bake

4 (10 ounce) cans whole asparagus, drained	4 (280 g)
3 eggs, hard-boiled, sliced	
2 tablespoons (1/4 stick) butter, melted	30 ml
1/3 cup milk	80 ml
1 1/2 cups shredded cheddar cheese	360 ml
1 1/4 cups cheese cracker crumbs	300 ml

• Place asparagus in buttered 7 x 11-inch (18 x 28 cm) baking dish. Arrange hard-boiled eggs on top and drizzle with butter.

• Pour milk over casserole.

• Sprinkle cheese on top, then add cracker crumbs.

• Bake uncovered at 350° (176° C) for 30 minutes.

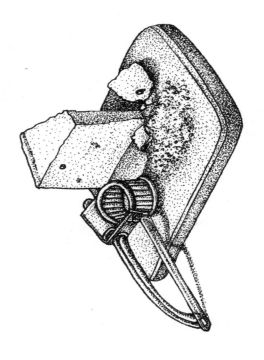

Swiss Asparagus

3 (15 ounce) cans asparagus spears, drained	3 (425 g)
1½ cups sour cream	360 ml
½ cup shredded Swiss cheese	120 ml
2 tablespoons minced onion flakes	30 ml
¼ teaspoon dry mustard	1 ml
¼ teaspoon garlic powder	1 ml
1 cup fresh breadcrumbs	240 ml
3 tablespoons butter, melted	45 ml

- Place asparagus in 1½-quart (1.5 L) buttered baking dish.

- Combine sour cream, Swiss cheese, onion flakes, ¾ teaspoon (4 ml) salt, ¼ teaspoon (1 ml) pepper, dry mustard and garlic powder and mix well to blend.

- Spoon sour cream mixture over asparagus.

- Toss breadcrumbs with melted butter and sprinkle over casserole.

- Bake uncovered at 325° (162° C) for 30 minutes.

Asparagus-Cheese Bake

3 (15 ounce) cans cut asparagus spears,
with liquid .... 3 (425 g)
3 hard-boiled eggs, chopped
½ cup chopped pecans .... 120 ml
1 (10 ounce) can cream of asparagus soup ... 280 g
¼ cup (½ stick) butter .... 60 ml
2 cups cracker crumbs .... 480 ml
1 (8 ounce) package shredded Monterey
Jack cheese .... 227 g

• Arrange drained asparagus spears in buttered, 2-quart
  (2 L) baking dish. Top with chopped eggs and pecans.

• Heat asparagus soup, liquid from asparagus, butter
  and some pepper. Pour over asparagus, eggs and
  pecans.

• Combine cracker crumbs and cheese. Sprinkle over
  casserole.

• Bake uncovered at 350° (176° C) for 25 minutes.

Baked Tomatoes

This is a really old recipe, but well worth reviving. People who had gardens always had plenty of tomatoes and this was their way of making a hot dish with tomatoes. Try it - you'll like it!

2 (15 ounce) cans diced tomatoes, drained	2 (425 g)	
1½ cups toasted breadcrumbs, divided	360 ml	
Scant ¼ cup sugar	60 ml	
½ onion, chopped		
¼ cup (½ stick) butter, melted	60 ml	

• Combine tomatoes, 1 cup (240 ml) breadcrumbs, sugar, ½ teaspoon (2 ml) salt, onion and butter.

• Pour into 2-quart (2 L) buttered baking dish and cover with remaining breadcrumbs.

• Bake uncovered at 325° (162° C).

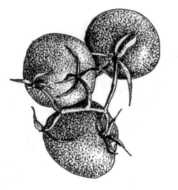

Black-Eyed Peas and Tomatoes

This dish is a "must" for Southerners on New Year's Day because eating black-eyed peas will bring good luck for the coming year!

1 bell pepper, seeded, chopped	
1 large onion, chopped	
2 ribs celery, chopped	
2 tablespoons (¼ stick) butter	30 ml
2 (15 ounce) can jalapeno black-eyed peas, drained	2 (425 g)
1 (15 ounce) can stewed tomatoes, with liquid	425 g
1 teaspoon garlic powder	5 ml
¼ cup ketchup	60 ml
2 teaspoons dry chicken bouillon	10 ml

- Saute bell pepper, onion and celery in butter to tender-crisp, but do not overcook.

- In bowl, combine pepper-celery mixture, black-eyed peas, stewed tomatoes, garlic powder, ketchup and chicken bouillon. Spoon into 2-quart (2 L) baking dish.

- Cover and bake at 350° (176° C) for about 20 minutes or just until it bubbles.

Crispy Gingered Peas

2 (10 ounce) packages frozen peas	2 (280 g)
3 tablespoons butter	45 ml
1 (6 ounce) can sliced mushrooms, drained	168 g
1 (8 ounce) can sliced water chestnuts, drained	227 g
1 bunch green onions, chopped	
1 (4 ounce) jar chopped pimento, drained	114 g
3/4 teaspoon ground ginger	4 ml
1/4 teaspoon nutmeg	1 ml
1 (14 ounce) can chicken broth, divided	396 g
2 tablespoons cornstarch	30 ml
1/4 teaspoon garlic powder	1 ml
3 tablespoons finely chopped crystallized ginger	45 ml

• Place peas, butter, mushrooms, water chestnuts, green onions, pimento, ginger, nutmeg and all but 1/4 cup (60 ml) chicken broth in large saucepan. Cover and simmer over low heat for 6 to 8 minutes.

• Blend cornstarch and reserved chicken broth until smooth. Stir into peas-mushroom mixture.

• Cook slowly, stirring constantly until liquid boils and thickens.

• Add 1/2 teaspoon (2 ml) salt, garlic powder and crystallized ginger and mix well.

• Pour into buttered 2-quart (2 L) baking dish and bake covered at 325° (162° C) for 20 minutes.

Crackered-Onion Casserole

3 cups round buttery cracker crumbs   710 ml
½ cup (1 stick) butter, melted, divided   120 ml
2 onions, thinly sliced
1 cup milk   240 ml
2 eggs, slightly beaten
1 (8 ounce) package shredded cheddar cheese   227 g

- Combine and mix cracker crumbs and half butter. Place in 9 x 13-inch (23 x 33 cm) baking dish and pat down.

- Saute onions in remaining butter. Spread onions over crust.

- Combine milk, eggs, cheese and a little salt and pepper in saucepan. Heat on low just until cheese melts. Pour sauce over onions.

- Bake uncovered at 300° (148° C) for 45 minutes or until knife inserted in center comes out clean.

Tip: Serve as a replacement for potatoes or rice.

Smiling Onions

6 onions, sliced	
1 sweet red bell pepper, sliced	
½ cup (1 stick) butter, divided	120 ml
1 (10 ounce) box frozen green peas, thawed	280 g
1 cup slivered almonds, toasted	240 ml
1 tablespoon cornstarch	15 ml
1½ cups half-and-half cream	360 ml
½ cup grated parmesan cheese	120 ml
5 strips bacon, cooked, crumbled	

- Saute onions and bell pepper in large skillet, in ¼ cup (60 ml) butter, but do not let onions brown. Add peas and almonds.

- Melt ¼ cup (60 ml) butter in saucepan, add cornstarch, 1 teaspoon (5 ml) each of salt and pepper and stir until smooth. Gradually stir in cream and parmesan cheese and cook, stirring constantly, until sauce thickens.

- Pour over onion mixture. Spoon into buttered 3-quart (3 L) baking dish.

- Cover and bake at 350° (176° C) for 30 minutes.

- Remove from oven and sprinkle crumbled bacon over top of casserole.

Mushroom-Onion Pie

1 large onion, halved , thinly sliced	
2 cups sliced fresh mushroom	480 ml
1 tablespoon olive oil	15 ml
4 eggs, slightly beaten	
1 (8 ounce) carton whipping cream	227 g
½ teaspoon thyme	2 ml
½ teaspoon basil	2 ml
1 (9-inch) frozen deep-pastry shell, thawed	23 cm

• Saute onion slices and mushrooms in oil and cook on low heat for about 10 minutes, but do not brown.

• In bowl, combine eggs, whipping cream, thyme, basil, 1½ teaspoon (7 ml) salt, 1 teaspoon (5 ml) pepper and pinch of nutmeg (if you have it) and mix well. Pour into onion-mushroom mixture and stir.

• Place pastry shell on baking sheet and pour in all ingredients.

• Bake uncovered at 350° (176° C) for 45 minutes or until center sets.

Creamy Vegetable Casserole

These are vegetables at their best!

1 (16 ounce) package frozen broccoli, carrots
  and cauliflower   .5 kg
1 (10 ounce) box frozen green peas   280 g
1 (10 ounce) can cream of mushroom soup   280 g
½ cup milk   120 ml
1 (8 ounce) carton spreadable garden-vegetable
  cream cheese   227 g
1 cup seasoned croutons, crushed   240 ml

- Cook all vegetables according to package directions, but don't overcook! Drain and place in large bowl.

- In saucepan, place soup, milk and cream cheese and heat just enough to mix easily.

- Pour into vegetable mixture and stir well.

- Spoon into 2-quart (2 L) baking dish. Sprinkle with croutons.

- Bake uncovered at 350° (176° C) for 25 minutes or until bubbly.

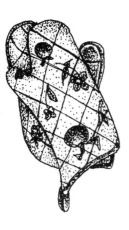

Absolutely Delicious Vegetables

2 (15 ounce) cans mixed vegetables, drained	2 (425 g)
1 cup celery, chopped	240 ml
½ onion, chopped	
1 (8 ounce) can sliced water chestnuts, drained	227 g
1 cup shredded sharp cheddar cheese	240 ml
¾ cup mayonnaise	180 ml
1½ cups round buttery crackers, crushed	360 ml
6 tablespoons (¾ stick) butter, melted	90 ml

- Combine vegetables, celery, onion, water chestnuts, cheese and mayonnaise in bowl and mix well. Spoon into buttered 9 x 13-inch (23 x 33 cm) baking dish.

- Combine crushed crackers and melted butter and sprinkle over vegetable mixture.

- Bake at 350° (176° C) for 30 minutes or until crackers are light brown.

Tip: *You will just have to make this dish to know how really good this recipe is. A friend at church started making this years ago and she always gets requests for these vegetables. Amazingly, you don't realize that it is loaded with vegetables. (What a great way to get your kids to eat vegetables!) The crispy top just sets it off and it couldn't be easier!*

Vegetable Frittata

This makes and elegant dish and is perfect for a brunch or late supper.

4 tablespoons light olive oil	60 ml
1 onion, chopped	
¾ cup green bell pepper, chopped	180 ml
¾ cup sweet red bell pepper, chopped	180 ml
2 cups chopped zucchini	240 ml
2 cups chopped yellow squash	240 ml
¼ cup half-and-half cream	60 ml
1 (8 ounce) package cream cheese, softened	227 g
6 eggs	
1 cup shredded mozzarella cheese	240 ml
¾ teaspoon garlic powder	4 ml
2 teaspoons white wine Worcestershire sauce	10 ml
1 cup seasoned breadcrumbs	240 ml
3 tablespoons butter, melted	45 ml

- Heat oil in large skillet. Saute onion, bell peppers, zucchini and squash just until tender-crisp. Remove from heat and set aside to cool.

- In mixing bowl, beat half-and-half with cream cheese until creamy. Add eggs and beat about 4 minutes until both mix well.

- Add mozzarella cheese, garlic powder, white wine Worcestershire and ½ teaspoon (2 ml) each of salt and pepper and mix by hand. (Do not use dark Worcestershire because it makes vegetables too dark.)

- Fold in breadcrumbs, melted butter and vegetables. Pour into greased 9-inch (23 cm) springform pan.

- Bake uncovered at 350° (176° C) for 55 to 60 minutes or until light brown and set in center.

- Set aside for 10 minutes before slicing to serve. (Be sure to use a thin, sharp knife to cut around the edge of the springform pan before you open the pan.)

The Veggie Patch

1 (10 ounce) can cream of chicken soup	280 g
1 (10 ounce) can cream of celery soup	280 g
½ cup milk	120 ml
1½ cups shredded cheddar cheese	360 ml
1 teaspoon dried basil	5 ml
1 (8 ounce) can whole kernel corn, drained	227 g
1 (16 ounce) package frozen broccoli florets, thawed, trimmed	.5 kg
1 (16 ounce) package frozen cauliflower, thawed	.5 kg
1 red and 1 green bell pepper, sliced	
1½ cups round butter cracker crumbs	360 ml
2 tablespoons butter, melted	30 ml

- Combine soups, milk, cheese, basil and a little salt and pepper in saucepan and heat just enough to pour.

- In buttered 3-quart (3 L) baking dish, combine corn, broccoli, cauliflower and bell peppers.

- Pour soup-cheese mixture over vegetables. Sprinkle buttered cracker crumbs over casserole.

- Bake uncovered at 325° (162° C) for about 35 minutes.

Tip: Have you got a slice of ham? Well, that's all you need to serve with these wonderfully seasoned vegetables to make a great meal.

Spicy Vegetable Couscous

1 (6 ounce) package herbed-chicken couscous	168 g	
3 tablespoons butter	45 ml	
3 tablespoons oil	45 ml	
1 small yellow squash, diced		
1 small zucchini, diced		
1/2 red onion, diced		
1 sweet red bell pepper, diced		
1 (10 ounce) box frozen green peas, thawed	280 g	
1/2 teaspoon garlic powder	2 ml	
1/2 teaspoon ground cumin	2 ml	
1/2 teaspoon curry powder	2 ml	
1/4 teaspoon cayenne pepper	1 ml	
1 1/2 cups shredded mozzarella cheese	360 ml	

- Cook couscous according to package directions, but add 3 tablespoons (45 ml) butter instead of amount specified.

- In large skillet, heat oil and saute squash, zucchini, onion and bell pepper for about 10 minutes, do not brown. Add peas, garlic powder, cumin, curry powder, cayenne pepper and 1/2 teaspoon (2 ml) salt and toss.

- Combine vegetables and couscous. If it seems a little dry, add a few tablespoons water.

- Pour into buttered 2 1/2-quart (2.5 L) baking dish and sprinkle with mozzarella cheese.

- Bake covered at 350° (176° C) for about 25 minutes.

Tip: This is really good, and a very colorful and attractive dish. This may be refrigerated and heated later. Allow it to sit at room temperature for about 30 minutes before heating. If you prefer a milder hot, use only 1/8 teaspoon (.5 ml) cayenne pepper.

104

Summer Pie

3 large tomatoes, peeled, sliced
1 (9-inch) deep-dish frozen piecrust, thawed   23 cm
4 bacon slices, cooked, drained, crumbled
1 tablespoon bacon drippings, reserved   15 ml
3 yellow onions, halved, thinly sliced
1 cup shredded cheddar cheese   240 ml
1 cup mayonnaise   240 ml
1 (3 ounce) package grated parmesan cheese   84 g
2 tablespoons seasoned breadcrumbs   30 ml

- Place tomatoes on paper towels and sprinkle with ½ teaspoon (2 ml) salt. Let stand 30 minutes.

- Place piecrust in deep-dish pie plate and crimp edges of crust.

- Bake at 400° (204° C) for about 10 minutes or until light brown.

- Saute onions in bacon drippings in large skillet. Spoon onion over prepared piecrust and top with tomato slices.

- In bowl, combine cheese, mayonnaise and pepper. Spread mixture over tomato slices.

- Combine parmesan cheese and breadcrumbs and sprinkle over top.

- Bake at 350° (176° C) for 30 minutes or until light brown.

- Sprinkle crumbled bacon over top of pie.

- Let stand 5 minutes before serving.

Awesome Butternut Casserole

2½ cups cooked, mashed butternut squash		600 ml
½ cup (1 stick) butter, melted, divided		120 ml
¾ cup sugar		180 ml
3 tablespoons brown sugar		45 ml
3 eggs, beaten		
1 (5 ounce) can evaporated milk		143 g
1 teaspoon vanilla		5 ml
½ teaspoon cinnamon		2 ml

- Place scooped-out squash in mixing bowl and beat until fairly smooth.

- Place 2½ cups (600 ml) mashed squash (discard extra squash) in large bowl. Add butter, sugar, brown sugar, eggs, milk, vanilla and cinnamon and mix well. Mixture will be thin. Pour into buttered 3-quart (3 L) baking dish.

- Bake uncovered at 350° (176° C) for 45 minutes or until almost set.

Topping:

1 cup crushed corn flakes		240 ml
½ cup packed light brown sugar		120 ml
½ cup chopped pecans		120 ml

- Combine topping ingredients, sprinkle over hot casserole and return to oven for 10 to 15 minutes or until top is crunchy.

Tip: The best way to cook a butternut squash is to cut the squash in half, scoop out seeds and membranes and place cut-side down on plate and microwave on HIGH for 1 to 2 minutes. Let stand in microwave for several minutes. If it is not soft enough, microwave 1 more minute.

Wraps Italienne

This is a fun dish to serve family or friends and goes with most meals.

1 (10 ounce) box frozen chopped spinach, thawed	280 g
1 (8 ounce) can whole kernel corn, drained	227 g
1 (15 ounce) carton ricotta cheese	425 g
1 egg	
2 (8 ounce) packages fancy shredded Italian-cheese blend, divided	2 (227 g)
8 flour tortillas	
1 (15 ounce) can Italian-style stewed tomatoes, with liquid	425 g
1 (8 ounce) can tomato sauce	227 g
1 teaspoon Italian seasoning	5 ml
1 teaspoon dried basil leaves	5 ml
1 (3 ounce) package grated parmesan cheese	84 g

• Press spinach into several paper towels to drain. Repeat to make sure spinach drains well.

• In medium bowl, combine spinach, corn, ricotta cheese, egg and 1 (8 ounce/227 g) package shredded Italian-cheese blend and mix well.

• Lay all tortillas on counter and place 1 heaping ¼ cup (60 ml) spinach mixture in center of each tortilla.

• Roll tightly and arrange seam-side down in greased 9 x 13-inch (23 x 33 cm) baking pan. Use same bowl to combine stewed tomatoes, tomato sauce, Italian seasoning, and a little salt and basil leaves. Spoon mixture over tortillas.

• Sprinkle with remaining Italian-cheese.

• Bake uncovered at 350° (176° C) for 30 minutes.

• Remove from oven and sprinkle parmesan cheese over top and return to oven for 5 minutes or just until parmesan melts.

Vegetables

Scalloped Potatoes

6 potatoes	
½ cup (1 stick) butter	120 ml
1 tablespoon flour	15 ml
¾ cup milk	180 ml
1 (8 ounce) package shredded cheddar cheese	227 g

• Peel and wash potatoes. Slice half of potatoes and place in 3-quart (3 L) greased baking dish.

• Slice butter and place half over potatoes.

• Sprinkle with a little pepper and flour.

• Slice remaining potatoes and place over first layer, add remaining butter slices and pour milk over casserole.

• Sprinkle with a little more pepper and cover with remaining cheese.

• Sprinkle flour over top of pepper. Cover with half cheese.

• Cover and bake at 350° (176° C) for 1 hour.

Tip: This must be cooked immediately or potatoes will darken. It can be frozen after baking and then reheated.

The Ultimate Potato

This is no time to count calories!

6 large baking potatoes, boiled	
1 cup light cream	240 ml
6 tablespoons (3/4 stick) butter	90 ml
1 (8 ounce) package shredded cheddar cheese	227 g
1 (8 ounce) carton sour cream	227 g
½ cup green onions, chopped	120 ml
6 strips bacon, fried, crumbled	

- Peel cooled potatoes and grate.

- Combine cream, butter, cheese and sour cream in double boiler and stir just until they melt.

- Add cheese mixture to grated potatoes and place in greased 4-quart (4 L) baking dish.

- Cover and bake at 350° (176° C) for 30 minutes.

- Top with onions and crumbled bacon to serve.

Glory Potatoes

Talk about a "good" potato, this is it! And you
don't have to peel a single potato.

1 (22 ounce) package frozen tater tots   624 g
2 eggs, beaten
1 (10 ounce) can cream of potato soup   280 g
1 (10 ounce) can cram of chicken soup   280 g
1 (8 ounce) carton sour cream   227 g
¾ cup milk   180 ml
½ teaspoon garlic powder
1 green and red bell pepper, thinly sliced
1 onion, chopped   2 ml
1 (12 ounce) package shredded cheddar cheese,
divided   340 g

- Butter 11 x 14-inch (30 x 36 cm) baking dish and arrange tater tots in casserole.

- In large bowl, combine eggs, both soups, sour cream, milk, both bell peppers, onion, 1 teaspoon (5 ml) each of salt and pepper and mix well.

- Fold in half cheddar cheese. Spoon mixture over tater tots.

- Bake covered at 350° (176° C) for 50 minutes or until bubbly.

- Remove from oven, sprinkle remaining cheese over casserole and return to oven for about 5 minutes.

New Potatoes With Herb Butter

1½ pounds new potatoes	680 g
2 tablespoon (¼ stick) butter, sliced	30 ml
¼ teaspoon thyme	1 ml
½ cup chopped fresh parsley	120 ml
½ teaspoon rosemary	2 ml

- Scrub potatoes and cut in halves unpeeled.

- In medium saucepan, boil potatoes in lightly salted water. Cook until potatoes are tender, about 15 minutes. Drain.

- Add butter, thyme, parsley and rosemary. Toss gently until butter melts.

Did you know that, on average, an American eats 124 pounds of potatoes per year?

Hallelujah Potatoes

This is a super baked potato!

6 baking potatoes
½ **cup (1 stick) butter**   120 ml
1 **(8 ounce) package cream cheese, softened**   227 g
1 **bunch fresh green onions, with tops, sliced**
1 **(6 ounce) can crabmeat, drained, flaked**   168 g
1 **cup shredded cheddar cheese**   240 ml

- Bake potatoes at 400° (204° C) for 1 hour or until done.

- Halve potatoes lengthwise, scoop out pulp and reserve skins.

- In mixing bowl, beat hot potatoes, butter, cream cheese, 1 teaspoon (5 ml) each of salt and pepper and beat well. Stir in onions and crabmeat.

- Fill reserved skins with potato mixture. Sprinkle cheese over top of potatoes.

- Place on baking sheet and bake at 350° (176° C) for 20 minutes or until it bubbles.

Cheddar-Potato Casserole

This is a "winner" for the best potato casserole you will ever make! It is a particular favorite of the men!

1 (2 pound) bag frozen hash brown potatoes, thawed	1 kg
1 onion, finely chopped	
¾ cup (1 stick) butter, melted, divided	180 ml
1 (8 ounce) carton sour cream	227 g
1 (10 ounce) can cream of chicken soup	280 g
1 (8 ounce) package shredded cheddar cheese	227 g
2 cups crushed corn flakes	480 ml

• Combine hash browns, onion, ½ cup (120 ml) butter, sour cream, soup and cheese in large mixing bowl and mix well.

• Pour into greased 9 x 13-inch (23 x 33 cm) baking dish.

• Combine corn flakes and ¼ cup (60 ml) melted butter. Sprinkle over top of casserole.

• Bake uncovered at 350° (176° C) for 45 to 50 minutes or until bubbly around edges.

Did you know that one out of every three meals in America contains a potato?

Bacon-Potato Casserole

4 pounds red, new potatoes, with peels	1.8 kg
1 pound sliced bacon, cooked, drained, crumbled, divided	.5 kg
1 (12 ounce) package shredded processed cheese	340 g
1 (8 ounce) package shredded Monterey Jack cheese, divided	227 g
2 onions, chopped	
1 (4 ounce) jar chopped pimentos, drained	114 g
1 cup mayonnaise	240 ml
1 (8 ounce) carton sour cream	227 g
1 tablespoon dried parsley flakes	15 ml
1 teaspoon basil	5 ml

- Cut potatoes in half and cook in boiling water with a little salt. Drain well.

- In very large bowl, combine potatoes, half crumbled bacon, processed cheese, half Jack cheese, 1 teaspoon (5 ml) each of salt and pepper and all remaining ingredients and mix well.

- Spoon into greased 11 x 14-inch (30 x 36 cm) baking dish, or smaller ones. (You may freeze one.)

- Bake uncovered at 325° (162° C) for 40 minutes or until edges bubbles.

- Remove from oven and sprinkle remaining Jack cheese over top of casserole. Return to oven for about 5 minutes, just until cheese melts.

- Before serving, sprinkle remaining crumbled bacon over top of casserole.

Mashed-Potatoes Supreme

1 (8 ounce) package cream cheese, softened	227 g
½ cup sour cream	120 ml
2 tablespoons (¼ stick) butter, softened	30 ml
1 (1 ounce) envelope ranch salad dressing	28 g
8-9 cups instant mashed potatoes, warmed	2 L

• With mixer, combine cream cheese, sour cream, butter and salad dressing and mix well. Add potatoes and stir well.

• Transfer to 1-quart (1 L) baking dish.

• Bake at 350° (176° C) for 25 minutes or until it is hot.

The Irish knew a good thing when they utilized the wonderful "potato". In a world where french-fries reign, the succulent potato is one of the most versatile of all vegetables.

Sweet Potato Casserole

This is a beautiful Thanksgiving dish and perfect for Christmas dinner too. Even people who are "like warm" about sweet potatoes like this casserole.

1 (29 ounce) can sweet potatoes, drained	805 g
¾ cup evaporated milk	80 ml
¼ cup sugar	180 ml
¼ cup packed brown sugar	60 ml
2 eggs, beaten	
¼ cup (½ stick) butter, melted	60 ml
1 teaspoon vanilla	5 ml

Topping:

1 cup packed light brown sugar	240 ml
¼ cup (½ stick) butter, melted	60 ml
½ cup flour	120 ml
1 cup chopped pecans	240 ml

- Place sweet potatoes in mixing bowl and mash slightly with fork.

- Add evaporated milk, sugar, eggs, butter and vanilla and mix well.

- Pour into greased 7 x 11-inch (18 x 28 cm) baking dish or a 2-quart (2 L) baking dish.

- For topping, combine brown sugar, butter and flour and mix well.

- Stir in chopped pecans and sprinkle topping over casserole.

- Bake uncovered at 350° (176° C) for 35 minutes or until crusty on top.

Sweet Potato Souffle

Happy holiday smiles get bigger when this dish is served.

2 (15 ounce) cans sweet potatoes, drained, mashed	2 (425 g)
2 cups sugar	480 ml
4 eggs, beaten	
1 cup half-and-half cream	240 ml
¼ cup (½ stick) butter, melted	60 ml
2 teaspoons vanilla	10 ml

Topping:

1½ cups corn flakes, crushed	360 ml
1 cup packed brown sugar	240 ml
2 tablespoons (¼ stick) butter, melted	30 ml
1 cup chopped pecans	240 ml
⅓ cup flaked coconut	80 ml

- Combine sweet potatoes, sugar, eggs, cream, butter, ½ teaspoon (2 ml) salt and vanilla and mix well. (Mixture may be thin.)

- Pour into buttered 2-quart (2 L) baking dish.

- For topping, combine all ingredients and mix well.

- Sprinkle topping mixture over casserole, cover and bake at 350° (176° C) for 45 minutes.

- Uncover and bake another 15 minutes or until center is firm and the topping is light brown.

Speedy Sweet Potatoes

2 (15 ounce) cans sweet potatoes, drained	2 (425 g)
1 (8 ounce) can crushed pineapple, with juice	227 g
½ cup chopped pecans	120 ml
2 cups packed brown sugar	240 ml
½ cup miniature marshmallows, divided	120 ml
Slight sprinkle of cinnamon and nutmeg	

• In 2-quart (2 L) microwave-safe dish, layer sweet potatoes, pinch of salt, pineapple, pecans, brown sugar and ¼ cup (60 ml) marshmallows.

• Cover loosely and microwave on HIGH for 5 to 6 minutes or until bubby around edges.

• Top with remaining marshmallows. Heat uncovered on high for 30 seconds or until marshmallows puff.

• Sprinkle just a little cinnamon and nutmeg over top of casserole.

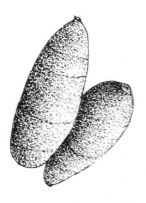

Chicken

Chicken Dish, WOW!

1 (10 ounce) can cream of chicken soup	280 g
1 (10 ounce) can fiesta nacho cheese	280 g
1 (5 ounce) can evaporated milk	143 g
2 (15 ounce) cans French-style green beans, drained	2 (425 g)
1 teaspoon chicken bouillon	5 ml
4 cups cooked, cubed chicken breasts	1 L
1 sweet red bell pepper, chopped	
2 ribs celery, sliced	
¼ cup onion, chopped	60 ml
1 cup chow mein noodles	240 ml
½ cup slivered almonds	120 ml
1 (3 ounce) can fried onion rings	84 g

- Combine soup, fiesta nacho cheese and evaporated milk and mix well.

- Fold in green beans, chicken bouillon, chicken, bell pepper, celery, onion, noodles, almonds, and ½ teaspoon (2 ml) each of salt and pepper.

- Spoon into buttered 9 x 13-inch (23 x 33 cm) baking dish.

- Bake covered at 350° (176° C) for 35 minutes. Remove from oven and sprinkle onion rings over casserole.

- Place back in oven and bake another 10 minutes.

Tip: This casserole may easily be made ahead of time and baked the next day. Just wait to add the onion rings until you put it in the oven.

Delightful Chicken Souffle

This is a fabulous dish for a luncheon. It is really easy to make and you may make it the day before the luncheon. Serve with an English pea salad and slice of cantaloupe or honey dew melon.

16 slices white bread, crusts removed
5 boneless, skinless, chicken breast halves, cooked,
　thinly sliced diagonally
½ cup mayonnaise   120 ml
1 cup shredded cheddar cheese, divided   240 ml
5 large eggs
2 cups milk   480 ml
1 (10 ounce) can cream of mushroom soup   280 g

• Butter 9 x 13-inch (23 x 33 cm) baking dish. Line bottom with 8 slices of bread, buttered on 1 side. Cover with sliced chicken.

• Spread chicken slices with mayonnaise and sprinkle with ½ cup (120 ml) cheese. Top with remaining 8 slices bread.

• Beat eggs, milk, ½ teaspoon (2 ml) each of salt and pepper and pour over entire casserole. Refrigerate all day or overnight.

• When ready to bake, spread mushroom soup with back of large spoon over top casserole.

• Bake covered at 350° (176° C) for 45 minutes.

• Uncover, sprinkle with remaining ½ cup (120 ml) cheddar cheese, return to oven and bake for another 15 minutes.

Tip: You could use deli-sliced chicken instead of cooking chicken breasts to save time.

Chicken and Tortilla Dumplings

These dumplings are wonderful. This recipe is actually easy. It just takes a little time to add tortilla strips, one at a time. Using tortillas are certainly a lot easier than making up biscuit dough for the dumplings!

6 large boneless, skinless chicken breasts
2 celery ribs, chopped
1 onion, chopped
2 tablespoons chicken bouillon   **30 ml**
1 (10 ounce) can cream of chicken soup   **280 g**
10-11 (8-inch) flour tortillas   **10-11 (20 cm)**

• Place chicken breasts, 10 cups (2 L) water, celery and onion in very large kettle or roaster. Bring to boil, reduce heat and cook about 30 minutes or until chicken is tender. Remove chicken and set aside to cool.

• Reserve broth in roaster. (You should have about 9 cups (2 L) of broth.) Add chicken bouillon and taste to make sure it is rich and tasty. Add more bouillon if needed and more water if you don't have 9 cups broth.

• When chicken is cool enough, cut into bite-size pieces and set aside.

• Add chicken soup to broth and bring to boil.

• Cut tortillas into 2 x 1-inch (5 x 2.5 cm) strips. Add strips, one at a time, to briskly boiling broth mixture and stir constantly.

• When all strips have been added, spoon in chicken, reduce heat to low and simmer 5 to 10 minutes. Stir well but gently, to prevent dumplings from sticking. Your kettle of chicken and dumplings will be very thick. Pour into very large serving bowl and serve hot.

One-Dish Chicken Bake

This is such a good, basic "meat and potato" dish that the family will love it. And for a change of pace, heat some hot, thick and chunky salsa to spoon over the top of each serving.

¼ cup (½ stick) butter	60 ml
1 sweet red bell pepper, chopped	
1 onion, chopped	
2 ribs celery, chopped	
1 (8 ounce) carton sour cream	227 g
1½ cups half-and-half cream	360 ml
1 (7 ounce) can chopped green chilies, drained	198 g
1 teaspoon chicken bouillon	5 ml
½ teaspoon celery salt	2 ml
3-4 cups cooked, cubed chicken	710-960 ml
1 (16 ounce) package shredded cheddar cheese, divided	.5 kg
1 (2 pound) package frozen hash brown potatoes, thawed	1 kg

• Melt butter in saucepan and saute bell pepper, onion and celery.

• In large bowl, combine sour cream, half-and-half, green chilies, seasonings and about ½ teaspoon (2 ml) each of salt and pepper. Stir in bell pepper mixture, chicken and half of cheese.

• Fold in hash brown potatoes. Spoon into greased 9 x 13-inch (23 x 33 cm) baking dish.

• Bake uncovered at 350° (176° C) for 45 minutes or until casserole bubbles.

• Remove from oven and sprinkle remaining cheese over top of casserole. Return to oven for about 5 minutes.

Three Cheers for Chicken

This chicken casserole is a meal in itself. Just add a tossed green salad and you have a completely, delicious, satisfying meal.

8 boneless, skinless chicken breast halves		
6 tablespoons (¾ stick) butter	90 ml	
1 cup celery, chopped	240 ml	
1 onion, chopped		
1 small bell pepper, chopped		
1 (4 ounce) jar chopped pimentos, drained	114 g	
1 cup uncooked rice	240 ml	
1 (10 ounce) can cream of chicken soup	280 g	
1 (10 ounce) can cream of celery soup	280 g	
2 soup cans milk		
1 (8 ounce) can sliced water chestnuts, drained	227 g	
1½ cups shredded cheddar cheese	360 ml	

• Place chicken breasts in large, greased 11 x 14-inch (30 x 36 cm) baking dish and sprinkle with a little salt and pepper.

• Melt butter in large skillet and saute celery, onion and bell pepper. Add pimentos, rice, soups, milk and water chestnuts and mix well.

• Pour mixture over chicken breasts.

• Cook chicken covered at 325° (162° C) for 60 minutes.

• Uncover and cook another 10 minutes.

• Remove from oven, sprinkle cheese over top of casserole and bake 5 minutes longer.

Mr. Mozz's Spaghetti

*This is a wonderful casserole to serve to family or for company.
It has great flavor and taste with chicken, pasta and colorful
vegetables all in one dish. It's a winner, I promise!*

1 bunch fresh green onions, with tops, chopped	
1 cup celery, chopped	
1 sweet red bell pepper, chopped	
1 yellow or orange bell pepper, chopped	
¼ cup (½ stick) butter	60 ml
1 tablespoon dried cilantro leaves	15 ml
1 teaspoon Italian seasoning	5 ml
1 (7 ounce) package thin spaghetti, cooked, drained	198 g
4 cups cooked chicken or turkey, chopped	1 L
1 (8 ounce) carton sour cream	227 g
1 (16 ounce) jar creamy alfredo sauce	.5 kg
1 (10 ounce) box frozen green peas, thawed	280 g
1 (8 ounce) package shredded mozzarella cheese, divided	227 g

- Saute onions, celery and bell peppers in large skillet with butter.

- In large bowl combine onion-pepper mixture, seasonings, a little salt and pepper, spaghetti, chicken, sour cream and alfredo sauce and mix well. Fold in peas and half mozzarella cheese.

- Spoon into greased 10 x 14-inch (25 cm x 36 cm) deep baking dish and bake covered at 350° (176° C) for 45 minutes.

- Remove from oven and sprinkle remaining cheese over casserole. Return to oven for about 5 minutes.

Tip: With spaghetti dishes like this, I like to break up the spaghetti before cooking it. It just makes it a little easier to serve and to eat.

Chicken-Cheese Enchiladas

1 (1 ounce) package taco seasoning	28 g	
2 tablespoons oil, divided	30 ml	
4-5 large boneless, skinless chicken breast halves		
1 (16 ounce) jar chunky salsa, divided	.5 kg	
1 (12 ounce) package shredded Monterey Jack cheese, divided	340 ml	
1 (15 ounce) carton ricotta cheese	425 g	
1 (4 ounce) can chopped green chilies	114 g	
1 egg		
1 teaspoon dried cilantro	5 ml	
1 (10 ounce) package flour tortillas	280 g	
Sour cream		

- Combine ¼ cup (60 ml) water, taco seasoning and 1 tablespoon (15 ml) oil in shallow bowl and mix well. Place seasoning mixture in plastic bag. Cut chicken breasts into bite-size pieces and place in bag with seasoning mix. Seal and refrigerate for 1 to 2 hours.

- Cook chicken in remaining oil over medium high heat for about 15 minutes. Combine ½ cup (120 ml) salsa and ¼ cup (60 ml) water and spoon into greased 9 x 13-inch (23 x 33 cm) baking dish. Spread evenly over bottom of dish.

- Stir together 2½ cups (600 ml) Monterey Jack cheese, ricotta cheese, green chilies, egg, cilantro and ½ teaspoon (2 ml) salt. Spoon ⅓ cup (80 ml) cheese mixture down center of each tortilla, top with chicken and roll.

- Place tortillas, seam-side down, over salsa mixture in dish.

- Drizzle remaining salsa over enchiladas and sprinkle with remaining ½ cup (120 ml) Monterey Jack cheese.

- Bake uncovered at 350° (176° C) for 25 minutes. To serve, top with a dab of sour cream.

Cheesy, Cheesy Chicken

Cheese lovers dig in! It's a winner!

1 onion, chopped	
1 red and ½ green bell pepper, chopped	
½ cup (1 stick) butter, divided	120 ml
1 (10 ounce) can cream of chicken soup	280 g
1 (4 ounce) can sliced mushrooms	114 g
½ teaspoon dried cilantro	2 ml
½ teaspoon dried basil	2 ml
1 teaspoon celery salt	5 ml
½ teaspoon garlic pepper	2 ml
1 (8 ounce) package egg noodles,	
cooked al dente, drained	227 g
4-5 boneless, skinless chicken breast halves,	
cooked, cubed	
1 (15 ounce) carton ricotta cheese	425 g
1 (16 ounce) package shredded cheddar cheese	.5 kg
⅓ cup grated parmesan cheese	80 ml
1 cup breadcrumbs	240 ml

- Saute onion and bell peppers with 5 tablespoons (75 ml) butter in skillet. Remove from heat and stir in soup, mushrooms, cilantro, basil, garlic pepper and a little salt.

- In large bowl combine noodles, chicken, cheeses and soup-mushroom mixture. Mix well.

- Spoon into buttered 9 x 13-inch (23 x 33 cm) baking dish.

- Melt 3 tablespoons (45 ml) butter and combine with breadcrumbs. Sprinkle over casserole.

- Bake covered at 350° (176° C) for 45 minutes.

Chicken-Sausage Extraordinaire

1 (6 ounce) box long grain, wild rice	168 g
1 pound pork sausage	.5 kg
1 cup celery, chopped	240 ml
2 onions, chopped	
1 (4 ounce) jar sliced mushrooms, drained	114 g
6 boneless, skinless, chicken breast halves, cooked, sliced	
4 tablespoons butter, divided	60 ml
¼ cup flour	60 ml
1 cup whipping cream	240 ml
1 (14 ounce) can chicken broth	396 ml
1 teaspoon poultry seasoning	5 ml
2 cups crushed crackers	480 ml

- Cook rice according to package directions and set aside.

- In skillet, brown sausage and remove with slotted spoon. Saute celery and onions in sausage fat until onion is transparent, but not brown. Drain.

- Stir in mushrooms and chicken and set aside.

- Melt 3 tablespoons (45 ml) butter in large saucepan, add flour and mix well.

- Over medium heat, slowly add cream, broth and poultry seasoning. Cook, stirring constantly, until mixture is fairly thick. Pour into large bowl.

(Continued on next page.)

Chicken

(Continued)

• Add rice, sausage-onion mixture, chicken-mushroom mixture and ½ teaspoon (2 ml) each of salt and pepper.

• Spoon into 10 x 14-inch (25 x 36 cm) buttered baking dish.

• Mix 1 tablespoon (15 ml) melted butter, crushed crackers and sprinkle over casserole.

• Bake uncovered at 350° (176° C) for 40 minutes or until bubbles around edges.

Tip: *This dish makes enough for about 12 to 14 people so it could easily be placed into 2 smaller baking dishes and one may be frozen. If frozen, thaw in refrigerator and make sure it is thawed in the middle before cooking. Add 5 minutes to cooking time because casserole will be cold.*

Jalapeno Chicken

1 onion, chopped	
1 bunch fresh green onions, chopped	
2 tablespoons butter	30 ml
1 (10 ounce) package frozen spinach, thawed, drained	280 g
6 jalapenos, seeded, chopped	
1 (8 ounce) carton sour cream	227 g
2 (10 ounce) cans cream of chicken soup	2 (280 g)
1 teaspoon ground cumin	5 ml
1 (12 ounce) package nacho cheese-flavored tortilla chips, slightly crushed	340 g
4-5 cups cooked, chopped chicken	1 L
1 (8 ounce) package shredded Mexican 4-cheese blend	227 g

- Saute onions in butter in skillet.

- Drain spinach with several paper towels and squeeze water out of spinach. Add spinach, jalapenos, sour cream, chicken soup, ½ teaspoon (2 ml) salt and ground cumin to onions and mix well.

- In greased 9 x 13-inch (23 x 33 cm) baking dish, layer half tortilla chips, half chicken, half spinach-soup mixture and cheese. Repeat layers, but without last layer of cheese.

- Bake covered at 350° (176° C) for 40 minutes.

- Uncover and sprinkle remaining cheese over top and return to oven for 4 minutes or just until cheese melts.

Tip: If you like, you may substitute 1 (7 ounce/198 g) can chopped green chilies for jalapenos. It will not be as hot. You may also substitute leftover turkey for chicken.

Divine Chicken Casserole

1 (16 ounce) package frozen broccoli spears, thawed	.5 kg
1 (10 ounce) box frozen broccoli spears, thawed	280 g
3 cups diced, cooked chicken	710 ml
1 (10 ounce) can cream of chicken soup	280 g
2 tablespoons milk	30 ml
½ cup mayonnaise	120 ml
2 teaspoons lemon juice	10 ml
1 cup shredded cheddar cheese	240 ml
1½ cups round buttery cracker crumbs	360 ml
3 tablespoons butter, melted	45 ml

• Cook broccoli according to package directions and drain. Cut some stems away and discard.

• Place broccoli spears in buttered 9 x 13-inch (23 x 33 cm) baking dish and sprinkle a little salt over broccoli. Cover with diced chicken.

• Combine soup, milk, mayonnaise, lemon juice, cheese and a little pepper in saucepan. Heat just enough to pour mixture over broccoli and chicken.

• Combine cracker crumbs and butter and sprinkle over casserole.

• Bake uncovered at 350° (176° C) for 35 to 40 minutes or until hot and bubbly.

Chicken Supreme

It is really delicious and "sooo" easy. It is a great meal in itself.

1 onion, chopped		
1 cup celery, sliced	240 ml	
3 tablespoons butter	45 ml	
4 cups diced, cooked chicken breasts	1 L	
1 (6 ounce) package long grain, wild rice, cooked, with seasoning packet	168 g	
1 (10 ounce) can cream of celery soup	280 g	
1 (10 ounce) can cream of chicken soup	280 g	
1 (4 ounce) jar pimentos	114 g	
2 (15 ounce) cans French-style green beans, drained	2 (425 g)	
1 cup slivered almonds	240 ml	
1 cup mayonnaise	240 ml	
2½ cups potato chips, lightly crushed	600 ml	

- Saute onion and celery in butter. In very large saucepan, combine onion-celery mixture, diced chicken, cooked rice, both soups, pimentos, green beans, almonds, mayonnaise, ½ teaspoon (2 ml) each of salt and pepper and mix well.

- Spoon into greased 10 x 14 inch (25 x 36 cm) deep baking dish. Sprinkle crushed potato chips over top of casserole.

- Bake uncovered at 350° (176° C) for 40 minutes or until potato chips are light brown.

Tip: This recipe is a great way to serve a lot of people (at least 14 to 15 servings). It may also be made with green peas instead of green beans. If you want to make in advance and freeze or just refrigerate for the next day, just wait until you are ready to cook the casserole before adding potato chips.

Mexican Chicken

2 cups tortilla chips, crushed	480 ml
4 boneless, skinless chicken breast halves, cooked	
1 (15 ounce) can garbanzo beans, drained	425 g
1 (15 ounce) can pinto beans, drained	425 g
1 (15 ounce) can whole kernel corn, drained	425 g
1 (16 ounce) jar hot salsa	.5 kg
1 chopped red onion	
2 teaspoons cumin	10 ml
1 teaspoon dried cilantro leaves	5 ml
1 green bell pepper, diced	
2 teaspoons minced garlic	10 ml
1 (8 ounce) package shredded Monterey Jack cheese	227 g
1 (8 ounce) package shredded sharp cheddar cheese	227 g

• Grease 9 x 13-inch (23 x 33 cm) baking dish and scatter crushed tortilla chips evenly in dish.

• Cut chicken breasts in thin slices. In large bowl, combine chicken, beans, corn, salsa, onion, cumin, cilantro leaves, bell pepper, garlic and 1 teaspoon (5 ml) salt and mix well.

• Spoon half of mixture evenly over chips.

• Combine cheeses, and sprinkle half over mixture. Cover with remaining half of chicken-bean mixture and remaining cheese.

• Bake uncovered at 350° (176° C) for 35 minutes. Let stand 10 minutes before serving. Garnish with tomato slices, sour cream and chopped fresh onions, if you like.

The Chicken Takes the Artichoke

6 boneless, skinned chicken breast halves	
7 tablespoons butter, divided	105 ml
1 (14 ounce) jar water-packed artichoke hearts, drained	396 g
1 (8 ounce) can sliced water chestnuts, drained	227 g
1/4 cup flour	60 ml
1/8 teaspoon ground nutmeg	.5 ml
1 teaspoon summer savory	5 ml
1 teaspoon dried thyme	5 ml
1 (14 ounce) can chicken broth	396 g
1/2 cup whipping cream	120 ml
1 cup grated Swiss cheese	240 ml
1 cup seasoned breadcrumbs	240 ml

• Brown chicken breasts in 2 tablespoons (30 ml) butter in skillet. Place chicken breasts in greased 9 x 13-inch (23 x 33 cm) baking dish.

• Cut each artichoke heart in half and place artichokes and water chestnuts around chicken.

• In saucepan, melt 3 tablespoons (45 ml) butter and stir in flour, 1/2 teaspoon (2 ml) pepper, nutmeg, summer savory and thyme until smooth and mix well.

• On medium high heat, gradually stir in broth and cook, stirring constantly, until broth thickens. Remove from heat and stir in cream and Swiss cheese. Blend until cheese melts and pour over chicken, artichokes and water chestnuts.

• Combine breadcrumbs and 2 tablespoons (30 ml) melted butter and sprinkle over top of casserole.

• Bake uncovered at 350° (176° C) for 35 minutes.

Creamy Chicken Bake

1 (8 ounce) package egg noodles	227 g
1 (16 ounce) package frozen broccoli florets, thawed, trimmed	.5 kg
¼ cup (½ stick) butter, melted	60 ml
1 (8 ounce) package shredded cheddar cheese	227 g
1 (10 ounce) can cream of chicken soup	280 g
1 cup half-and-half cream	240 ml
¼ teaspoon ground mustard	1 ml
3 cups cooked, cubed chicken breasts	710 ml
⅔ cup slivered almonds, toasted	160 ml

• Cook noodles according to package directions and drain; keep warm.

• Combine noodles and broccoli in large bowl.

• Add butter and cheese and stir until cheese melts.

• Stir in chicken soup, cream, mustard, chicken and 1 teaspoon (5 ml) each of salt and pepper. Spoon into buttered 2½-quart (2.5 L) baking dish.

• Bake covered at 325° (162° C) for about 25 minutes.

• Remove from oven and sprinkle with slivered almonds and cool for 15 minutes longer.

Chicken-Noodle Delight

This recipe is a hearty main dish and the bell peppers make it colorful as well. It's a great family supper.

2 ribs celery, chopped	
½ onion, chopped	
½ green and ½ red bell pepper, chopped	
6 tablespoons (⅓ stick) butter, divided	90 ml
3 cups cooked, cubed chicken breasts	710 ml
1 (4 ounce) can sliced mushrooms, drained	114 g
1 (16 ounce) jar sun-dried tomato alfredo sauce	
½ cup half-and-half cream	.5 kg
1½ teaspoons chicken bouillon	120 ml
1 (8 ounce) package medium egg noodles, cooked, drained	7 ml
	227 g

Topping:

1 cup corn flake crumbs	240 ml
½ cup shredded cheddar cheese	120 ml

• Combine celery, onion, both bell peppers and 4 tablespoon (60 ml) butter in skillet or large saucepan and saute for about 5 minutes.

• Remove from heat and add chicken, mushrooms, alfredo sauce, cream, chicken bouillon and noodles and mix well.

• Pour into buttered 3-quart (3 L) baking dish.

• Combine topping ingredients and sprinkle over casserole.

• Bake uncovered at 325° (162° C) for 20 minutes or until casserole bubbles around edges.

Jolly Ole Chicken

*With this casserole you have the chicken and
cranberry sauce all in one dish.*

1 (6 ounce) package long grain, wild rice, with seasonings	168 g
1 (16 ounce) can whole berry cranberry sauce	.5 kg
⅓ cup orange juice	80 ml
3 tablespoons butter, melted	45 ml
½ teaspoon curry powder	2 ml
6-8 boneless, skinless chicken breast halves	
⅔ cup slivered almonds	160 ml

- Cook rice according to package directions and pour into greased 9 x 13-inch (23 x 33 cm) baking dish.

- Combine cranberry sauce, orange juice, butter and curry powder in saucepan and heat just enough to mix ingredients well.

- Place chicken breasts over rice and pour cranberry-orange juice mixture over chicken.

- Bake covered at 325° (162° C) for about 10 to 15 minutes.

- Uncover and sprinkle almonds over casserole and return to oven for about 10 to 15 minutes, just until chicken browns lightly.

Lemon-Almond Chicken

*Asparagus, lemon juice, curry powder and almonds
give a flavorful punch to this chicken dish.*

2 (14 ounce) cans cut asparagus, well drained	2 (396 g)	
4 boneless, skinless chicken breast halves, cut into ½-inch/1.2 cm strips		
3 tablespoons butter	45 ml	
1 (10 ounce) can cream of asparagus soup	280 g	
⅔ cup mayonnaise	160 ml	
¼ cup milk	60 ml	
1 sweet red bell pepper, julienned		
2 tablespoons lemon juice	30 ml	
1 teaspoon curry powder	5 ml	
¼ teaspoon ground ginger	1 ml	
½ cup sliced almonds, toasted	120 ml	

- Place asparagus in buttered 7 x 11-inch (18 x 28 cm) baking dish and set aside.

- Sprinkle chicken with ½ teaspoon (2 ml) salt.

- In large skillet, saute chicken in butter for about 15 minutes. Spoon chicken strips over asparagus.

- In skillet, combine asparagus soup, mayonnaise, milk, sweet red bell pepper, lemon juice, curry powder, ginger and ¼ teaspoon (1 ml) pepper and heat just enough to mix well.

- Spoon over chicken and sprinkle almonds over top of casserole.

- Bake uncovered at 350° (176° C) for 35 minutes.

Supper-Ready Chicken

Within 20 minutes you will have creamy chicken plus vegetables ready to go in the oven. And the kids will love the crunchy topping.

6 boneless, skinless chicken breast halves	
2 tablespoons oil	30 ml
1 cup celery, chopped	240 ml
2 cups sliced zucchini, ½-inch thick (1.2 cm)	480 ml
1 (16 ounce) package baby carrots	.5 kg
½ onion, chopped	
¼ cup (½ stick) plus 2 tablespoons butter	60 ml; 30 ml
1 (10 ounce) can cream of chicken soup	280 g
1 (10 ounce) can fiesta nacho cheese soup	280 g
1 cup milk or half-and-half cream	240 ml
½ teaspoon prepared mustard	2 ml
½ teaspoon dillweed	2 ml
1 teaspoon dried basil	5 ml
1½ cups soft breadcrumbs or cracker crumbs	360 ml
½ cup chopped walnuts	120 ml

- Brown chicken in skillet with oil. Place chicken breasts in greased 9 x 13-inch (23 x 33 cm) baking dish and set aside.

- In saucepan, cook celery, zucchini, carrots and onion for about 10 minutes in ¼ cup (60 ml) butter and very little water and drain.

- In saucepan, combine soups, milk, mustard, dill weed, basil and ½ teaspoon (2 ml) pepper and heat just enough to mix well. Spoon about ¾ cup (180 ml) soup mixture over chicken.

- Combine remaining soup mixture and drained vegetables. Spoon over chicken and soup mixture. Combine 2 tablespoons (30 ml) butter, breadcrumbs and walnuts and sprinkle over casserole.

- Bake uncovered at 375° (190° C) for 35 to 40 minutes or until topping browns lightly.

Spiced Spanish Chicken

2 cups instant rice, uncooked   480 ml
4 boneless, skinless, cooked
  chicken breast halves, cut into strips
1 (15 ounce) can Mexican-style
  stewed tomatoes, with juice   425 g
1 (8 ounce) can tomato sauce   227 g
1 (15 ounce) can whole kernel corn, drained   425 g
1 (4 ounce) jar diced pimentos, drained   114 g
1 teaspoon chili powder   5 ml
1 teaspoon ground cumin   5 ml

• Grease 3-quart (3 L) baking dish and spread rice
  evenly over dish. Place chicken strips over top of rice.

• In large bowl, combine stewed tomatoes, tomato
  sauce, corn, pimentos, chili powder, cumin,
  ½ teaspoon (2 ml) each of salt and pepper or cayenne
  pepper and mix well.

• Slowly and easily pour this mixture over chicken and
  rice.

• Bake covered at 350° (176° C) for 1 hour.

*Tip: The first time you try this, you might want to only ¼ teaspoon
       (1 ml) cayenne pepper, unless you know for sure you are prepared
       for "hot."*

Chicken Tetrazzini

½ cup (1 stick) butter	120 ml
6 tablespoons flour	90 ml
2 (14 ounce) cans chicken broth	2 (396 g)
1 (8 ounce) carton whipping cream	227 g
1 (16 ounce) package linguine, cooked, drained	
5-6 boneless, skinless chicken breast halves, cooked, cubed	.5 kg
1 cup sliced fresh mushrooms	240 ml
2 ribs celery, chopped	
1 green bell pepper, chopped	
1 (4 ounce) jar diced pimentos, drained	114 g
4-5 drops hot sauce	
½ cup grated parmesan cheese	120 ml

• Melt butter, add flour, a little salt and pepper in saucepan over medium heat and stir until smooth. Gradually add broth and bring to boil. Cook and stir constantly until it thickens.

• Remove from heat and stir in cream. If sauce seems too thick, add a little milk.

• Mix 2 cups (480 ml) sauce with linguine, pour into buttered 9 x 13-inch (23 x 33 cm) baking dish and spread over casserole dish.

• To remaining sauce, add chicken, mushrooms, celery, bell pepper, pimentos and hot sauce and mix well. Pour over linguine and sprinkle with parmesan cheese.

• Cover and bake at 350° (176° C) for about 45 minutes.

• Uncover and bake another 10 minutes.

Tip: You may use leftover turkey instead of chicken as long as the turkey is not smoked turkey. The white meat of the turkey is of course better to use than the dark meat.

Three-Cheese Chicken Casserole

1 (8 ounce) package small egg noodles	227 g
3 tablespoons butter	45 ml
1 green and 1 red bell pepper, chopped	
½ cup celery, chopped	120 ml
½ cup onion, chopped	120 ml
1 (10 ounce) can cream of chicken soup	280 g
½ cup milk	120 ml
1 (6 ounce) jar sliced mushrooms, drained	168 g
1 (12 ounce) carton small curd cottage cheese, drained	340 g
4 cups, cooked, diced chicken breasts, or turkey breasts	1 L
1 (12 ounce) package shredded cheddar cheese	340 g
¾ cup freshly grated parmesan	180 ml

- Cook noodles according to package directions and drain.

- Melt butter in skillet and saute peppers, celery and onion.

- In large bowl, combine noodles, sauteed mixture, chicken soup, milk, mushrooms, ½ teaspoon (2 ml) pepper, cottage cheese, chicken and cheddar cheese. Pour into sprayed 9 x 13-inch (23 x 33 cm) baking dish.

- Bake covered at 325° (162° C) for 35 to 40 minutes or until it bubbles around edges of casserole.

- Remove from oven, sprinkle parmesan cheese over casserole and return to oven for 5 minutes.

South-of-the-Border Chicken

This is really a delicious chicken dish, but it is spicy so be prepared. You need a tossed green salad garnished with avocado slices to complete this delicious meal.

8 boneless, skinless chicken breast, halves	
1 cup grated Monterey Jack cheese	240 ml
½ cup shredded cheddar cheese	120 ml
1 (4 ounce) can chopped green chilies	114 g
3 tablespoons dried onions	45 ml
½ cup (1 stick) butter	120 ml
2 teaspoons cumin	10 ml
1 teaspoon chili powder	5 ml
Tortilla chips, crushed	
Cooked white rice	

• Pound chicken breasts flat.

• Mix both cheeses, chilies and onions in bowl. Place 2 tablespoons (30 ml) cheese mixture on each chicken breast, roll and place seam-side down in greased 9 x 13-inch (23 x 33 cm) baking dish.

• Melt butter in saucepan, add cumin and chili powder and mix well. Pour over chicken.

• Bake covered at 350° (176° C) for 45 minutes.

• When chicken has 5 minutes left to cook, remove from oven, uncover and top with crushed chips. Return to oven and bake 5 more minutes. Serve over hot cooked rice.

Walnut Chicken

1 (6 ounce) box long grain, wild rice with herbs and seasonings	168 g
	480 ml
2 cups celery, chopped	480 ml
1 onion, chopped	
1 cup coarsely chopped walnuts	240 ml
2 tablespoons butter	30 ml
2 cups mayonnaise	480 ml
1 (8 ounce) carton sour cream	227 g
1 tablespoon lemon juice	15 ml
4 cups cooked, cubed chicken	1 L
1 cup potato chips, crushed	240 ml
1 (3 ounce) can fried onion rings, crushed	84 g

• Cook rice according to package directions.

• In skillet, lightly saute celery, onion and walnuts in butter. Add mayonnaise, sour cream, lemon juice, 3/4 teaspoon (4 ml) salt and chicken and mix well.

• Fold in cooked rice and transfer to greased 9 x 13-inch (23 x 33 cm) baking dish.

• Combine potato chips and crushed onion rings and sprinkle over top of casserole.

• Bake uncovered at 325° (162° C) for 25 minutes.

Comfort Chicken Plus

1 (6 ounce) box chicken stuffing mix	168 g
1 bunch fresh broccoli, cut into florets	
1 cup celery, chopped	240 ml
1 cup red bell pepper, chopped	240 ml
2 tablespoons butter	30 ml
1 (8 ounce) can whole kernel corn, drained	227 g
2½ cups finely chopped chicken or leftover turkey	600 ml
1 (1 ounce) envelope hollandaise sauce mix	28 g
1 (3 ounce) can french-fried onions	84 g

- Prepare chicken stuffing mix according to package directions.

- Place broccoli, celery, bell pepper, butter and ¼ cup (60 ml) water in microwave-safe bowl. Cover with wax paper and microwave on HIGH for 1½ minutes.

- Add broccoli-celery mixture, corn and chicken to stuffing and mix well. Spoon into buttered 8 x 12-inch (20 x 32 cm) baking dish.

- Prepare hollandaise sauce according to package directions, but use 1¼ cups (300 ml) water instead of 1 cup (240 ml) water stated.

- Pour hollandaise sauce over casserole and sprinkle top with onions.

- Bake uncovered at 325° (162° C) for 25 minutes.

Chicken Fiesta

This is another dish that leftover turkey may be substituted. You may put this recipe together in a matter of minutes. Basically, it involves chopping onion and bell peppers, opening 3 cans and a bag of chips. About 40 minutes later, you have a steaming hot, delicious casserole.

1 (13 ounce) bag tortilla chips	370 g	
4 cups cooked, chopped chicken breasts	1 L	
1 onion, chopped		
1 green and 1 red bell pepper, chopped		
1 (12 ounce) package shredded Mexican 4-cheese blend		
1 teaspoon chili powder		
½ teaspoon ground cumin		
2 (10 ounce) cans cream of chicken soup	340 g	
1 (10 ounce) can diced green chilies and tomatoes	280 g	

- Pour about two-thirds of tortilla chips into sprayed 9 x 13-inch (23 x 33 cm) baking dish and crush slightly with palm of your hand.

- In large bowl, combine chicken, onion, peppers, cheese, soup, tomatoes, chili powder, cumin and ½ teaspoon (2 ml) each of salt and pepper and mix well. Spoon mixture over crushed tortilla chips.

- Crush remaining tortilla chips in plastic bag and spread over casserole.

- Bake uncovered at 325° (162° C) for 40 minutes.

Chicken-Orzo Florentine

4 boneless, skinless chicken breast halves	
¾ cup uncooked orzo	180 ml
1 (8 ounce) package fresh mushrooms, sliced	227 g
1 (10 ounce) package frozen spinach, thawed, well drained	280 g
1 (10 ounce) can golden mushroom soup	280 g
½ cup mayonnaise	120 ml
1 tablespoon lemon juice	15 ml
1 (8 ounce) package Monterey Jack cheese	227 g
½ cup seasoned Italian breadcrumbs	120 ml

• Cook chicken in boiling water for about 15 minutes and reserve broth. Cut chicken in bite-size pieces and set aside.

• Pour broth through strainer and cook orzo in remaining broth.

• In large, sprayed skillet, saute mushrooms until tender. Remove from heat and stir in chicken, orzo, spinach, soup, mayonnaise, lemon juice and ½ teaspoon (2 ml) pepper.

• Fold in half cheese and mix well.

• Pour into greased 9 x 13-inch (23 x 33 cm) baking dish and sprinkle with remaining cheese and breadcrumbs.

• Bake uncovered at 350° (176° C) for 35 minutes.

Chicken-Broccoli Deluxe

½ cup (1 stick) butter	120 ml
½ cup flour	120 ml
1 (14 ounce) can chicken broth	396 g
1 pint half-and-half cream	.5 kg
1 (16 ounce) package shredded cheddar cheese, divided	.5 kg
1 (3 ounce) package fresh parmesan cheese, grated	84 g
2 tablespoons lemon juice	30 ml
1 tablespoon prepared mustard	15 ml
2 tablespoons dried parsley	30 ml
1 tablespoon dried onion flakes	15 ml
½ teaspoon basil	2 ml
¾ cup mayonnaise	180 ml
2 (10 ounce) boxes frozen broccoli florets, slightly cooked	2 (280 g)
5 chicken breast halves, cooked, sliced	
1 (7 ounce) box vermicelli	198 g

- Melt butter in very large saucepan or roaster. Add flour and mix.

- Over low to medium heat, gradually add chicken broth and cream, stirring constantly, until it thickens, but do not boil.

- Add half cheddar cheese, parmesan cheese, lemon juice, mustard, dried parsley, onion flakes, basil and 1 teaspoon (5 ml) salt and ½ teaspoon (2 ml) pepper. Heat on low until cheeses melt. Remove from heat and add mayonnaise.

(Continued on next page.)

Chicken

(Continued)

• Punch small holes in broccoli boxes and microwave 4 minutes. Do not over-cook. Gently add broccoli and chicken slices to sauce.

• Cook vermicelli according to package directions, drain and pour into greased 10 x 14-inch (25 x 36 cm) baking dish.

• Spoon sauce and chicken mixture over vermicelli.

• Bake covered at 325° (162° C) for 40 minutes.

• Uncover, spread remaining cheese over top. Return to oven for another 5 minutes.

Tip: This is another recipe that will serve a lot of hungry people and you may want to divide the ingredients in 2 smaller casseroles. One casserole may be frozen and cooked at a later date. Thaw in refrigerator and make sure it is thawed in the middle before cooking. Add 5 minutes to cooking time.

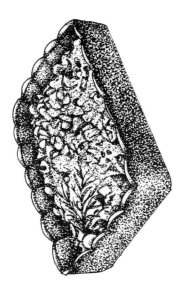

Chicken-Vegetable Medley

¼ cup (½ stick) plus	60 ml
3 tablespoons butter	45 ml
¼ cup flour	60 ml
1 pint half-and-half cream	.5 kg
½ cup cooking sherry	120 ml
1 (10 ounce) can cream of chicken soup	280 g
1 (10 ounce) package frozen broccoli spears, thawed	280 g
1 (10 ounce) package frozen cauliflower, thawed	280 g
1 sweet red bell pepper, thinly sliced	
1 cup celery, chopped	240 ml
1 cup cooked brown rice	240 ml
4 cups cooked, cubed chicken or turkey	1 L
1 (8 ounce) package shredded cheddar cheese	227 g
1 cup soft breadcrumbs	240 ml

- In saucepan, melt ¼ cup (60 ml) butter in saucepan, add flour and stir until they blend.

- Slowly stir in cream and sherry and cook, stirring constantly, until mixture thickens. Blend in soup until mixture is smooth and set aside.

- Place broccoli, cauliflower, red bell pepper and celery into buttered 9 x 13-inch (23 x 33 cm) baking dish.

- Cover with rice, half sauce and top with chicken. Stir shredded cheese into remaining sauce and pour over chicken.

- Melt 3 tablespoons (45 ml) butter and combine breadcrumbs. Sprinkle over casserole.

- Bake uncovered at 350° (176° C) for about 40 minutes or until casserole is hot.

Hurry-Up Chicken Enchiladas

This is a fast and fun way to make a dish with ingredients at your finger tips and it is a great dish for the kids to make.

2½-3 cups cooked, shredded
chicken breasts   600 ml;710 ml
1 (10 ounce) can cream of chicken soup   280 g
2 cups chunky salsa, divided   480 ml
8 (6-inch) flour tortillas   8 (15 cm)
1 (10 ounce) can fiesta nacho cheese soup   280 g

• Combine chicken (or substitute turkey), soup and ½ cup (120 ml) salsa in saucepan. Heat on low and stir constantly so mixture will not burn.

• Spread flour tortillas out on your counter and spoon about ⅓ cup (80 ml) chicken mixture on each tortilla.

• Roll tortilla around filling and place, seam-side down, in buttered 9 x 13-inch (23 x 33 cm) baking dish.

• In saucepan, combine nacho cheese, remaining salsa and ¼ cup (60 ml) water and heat just enough to pour mixture. Pour over enchiladas.

• Cover with wax paper and microwave on HIGH, turning several times, for 4-5 minutes or until it bubbles.

Chicken Martinez

1 (10 ounce) can fiesta nacho cheese soup	280 g
1 (10 ounce) can cream of chicken soup	280 g
1 (8 ounce) carton sour cream	227 g
1 onion, chopped	
1 (10 ounce) can diced tomatoes and green chilies	
1 (15 ounce) can black beans, rinsed, drained	425 g
1 (15 ounce) can whole kernel Mexicorn, drained	425 g
1 teaspoon chili powder	5 ml
8 flour tortillas, cut into strips	
4-5 large boneless, skinless chicken breast halves, cooked, cut into strips	
1 (8 ounce) package shredded Mexican 4-cheese blend	227 g

- Combine both soups, sour cream, onion, tomatoes, black beans, corn and chili powder in large bowl and mix well.

- Spread small amount of soup-bean mixture over bottom of greased 9 x 13-inch (23 x 33 cm) baking dish.

- Arrange half of tortilla strips over soup-bean mixture, a layer of chicken, another layer of soup-bean mixture, remaining tortilla strips and remaining chicken. Top with remaining soup-bean mixture.

- Bake covered 350° (176° C) for 45 minutes or until it bubbles.

- Uncover and spread shredded cheese over top of casserole. Return to oven for about 5 minutes, just until cheese melts.

Sweet Pepper Chicken

6-8 boneless, skinless chicken breasts halves	
2 tablespoons oil	30 ml
⅓ cup cornstarch	80 ml
⅔ cup sugar	160 ml
½ cup packed brown sugar	120 ml
1 teaspoon chicken bouillon granules	5 ml
1 (15 ounce) can pineapple chunks, with juice	425 g
1½ cups orange juice	360 ml
½ cup vinegar	120 ml
¼ cup ketchup	60 ml
2 tablespoons soy sauce	30 ml
¼ teaspoon ground ginger	1 ml
1 sweet red bell pepper, thinly sliced	

• Brown chicken breasts in large skillet with oil in large skillet. Place in buttered 10 x 14-inch (25 x 36 cm) baking dish.

• In large saucepan, combine cornstarch, sugar, brown sugar and bouillon granules and mix well.

• Drain pineapple and save juice. Add pineapple juice, orange juice, vinegar, ketchup, soy sauce and ginger to the cornstarch mixture in saucepan and mix well.

• Cook on high heat, stirring constantly, until mixture thickens. Pour sauce over chicken breasts.

• Bake uncovered at 325° (162° C) for 45 minutes.

• Remove from oven, add pineapple chunks and thinly sliced bell peppers and bake another 15 minutes.

Garden Chicken

This colorful, delicious casserole is not only flavor packed, but it is also a sight to behold! You can't beat this bountiful dish for family or company.

4 boneless, skinless chicken breasts halves, cut into strips		
1 teaspoon minced garlic	5 ml	
5 tablespoons butter, divided	75 ml	
1 small yellow squash, thinly sliced		
1 small zucchini, thinly sliced		
1 sweet red bell pepper, thinly sliced		
4 tablespoons flour		
2 teaspoons pesto seasoning		
1 (14 ounce) can chicken broth	396 g	
1 cup half-and-half cream	240 ml	
1 (8 ounce) package angel hair pasta, cooked al dente, drained	227 g	
⅓ cup shredded parmesan cheese	80 ml	

- Saute chicken and garlic in butter in large skillet over medium heat for about 15 minutes. Remove chicken and set aside.

- With butter in skillet, saute squash, zucchini and sweet bell pepper and cook just until tender-crisp.

- In small saucepan, melt 3 tablespoons (45 ml) butter and add flour, pesto seasoning and ½ teaspoon (2 ml) each of salt and pepper. Stir to form smooth paste.

(Continued on next page.)

Chicken

(Continued)

• Over medium high heat, gradually add broth, stirring constantly, until thick. Stir in cream and heat thoroughly.

• In large bowl, combine chicken, vegetables, broth-cream mixture and drained pasta. Transfer to greased 9 x 13-inch (23 x 33 cm) baking dish.

• Cover and bake at 350° (176° C) for 30 minutes.

• Uncover and sprinkle parmesan cheese over top of casserole and return to oven for another 5 minutes.

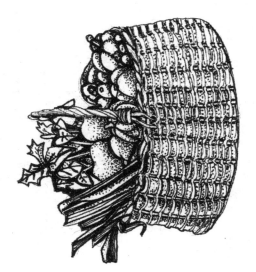

Orange-Spiced Chicken

⅔ cup flour		160 ml
½ teaspoon dried basil		2 ml
¼ teaspoon dried oregano		1 ml
¼ teaspoon marjoram		1 ml
¼ teaspoon leaf tarragon		1 ml
3 tablespoons oil		45 ml
6 boneless, skinless chicken breast halves		
1 (6 ounce) can frozen orange juice concentrate, thawed		168 g
½ cup white wine vinegar		120 ml
⅔ cup packed brown sugar		160 ml
1 (6 ounce) box long grain, wild rice		168 g

- Mix flour, spices and ½ teaspoon (2 ml) each of salt and pepper in plastic bag.

- Pour oil into large skillet and heat. Coat chicken in flour mixture, 1 or 2 pieces at a time. Brown both sides of chicken breasts in skillet.

- Place browned chicken breasts in greased 9 x 13-inch (23 x 33 cm) baking dish.

- In small bowl combine orange juice concentrate, ½ cup (120 ml) water, vinegar and brown sugar and mix well.

- Spoon about one-half of orange juice mixture over chicken breasts and bake uncovered at 325° (162° C) for 30 minutes.

- While chicken cooks, prepare rice according to package directions and spoon into second 9 x 13-inch (23 x 33 cm) baking dish.

- Place cooked chicken breasts over rice and pour remaining orange juice sauce over top of chicken.

Speedy Chicken Pie

Lunch for the girls is not only "speedy", it allows you extra minutes to create a special "out-a-sight" dessert.

1 (12 ounce) package shredded cheddar cheese, divided	340 g
1 (10 ounce) package frozen, chopped broccoli, thawed, drained	280 g
2 cups cooked, finely diced chicken breasts	480 ml
½ cup onion, finely chopped	120 ml
½ cup sweet red bell pepper, finely chopped	120 ml
1⅓ cups half-and-half cream	320 ml
3 eggs	
¾ cup biscuit mix	180 ml

• Combine 2 cups (480 ml) cheddar cheese, broccoli, chicken, onion and bell pepper in bowl. Spread into buttered deep 10-inch (25 cm) deep-dish pie plate.

• In mixing bowl, beat cream, eggs, baking mix, 1 teaspoon (5 ml) salt and ½ teaspoon (2 ml) pepper and mix well. Slowly pour cream-egg mixture over broccoli-chicken mixture, but do not stir.

• Bake covered at 375° (190° C) for 35 minutes or until center of pie is firm.

• Uncover and sprinkle remaining cheese over top. Return to oven for about 5 minutes or just until cheese melts.

Great Crazy Lasagna

Chicken never got mixed up with any better ingredients!

1 tablespoon butter	15 ml
1/2 onion, chopped	
1 cup fresh mushrooms, sliced	240 ml
1 (10 ounce) can cream of chicken soup	280 g
1 (16 ounce) jar alfredo sauce	.5 kg
1 (4 ounce) jar diced pimentos, drained	114 g
1/3 cup dry white wine	80 ml
1/2 teaspoon dried basil	2 ml
1 (10 ounce) package frozen chopped spinach, thawed	280 g
1 (15 ounce) carton ricotta cheese	425 g
1/3 cup grated parmesan cheese	80 ml
1 egg, beaten	
9 lasagna noodles, cooked	
3-4 cups cooked chicken, shredded	
1 (16 ounce) package shredded cheddar cheese	.5 kg
	1 L

- Melt butter and saute onion and mushrooms in large skillet. Stir in soup, alfredo sauce, pimentos, wine and basil. Reserve one-third sauce for top of lasagna.

- Drain spinach well, between several layers of paper towels. (The spinach needs to be completely drained.)

- In bowl, combine spinach, ricotta, parmesan and egg and mix well.

- Spray 10 x 15-inch (25 x 38 cm) baking dish with non-stick cooking spray and place 3 noodles in dish. Make sure 10 x 15-inch (25 x 38 cm) dish is full size with a depth of 2½ inches (6.5 cm).

(Continued on next page.)

(Continued)

- Layer each with half of remaining sauce, spinach-ricotta mixture and chicken. (The spinach-ricotta mixture will be fairly dry and you will have to pour it over sauce and spread out.)

- Sprinkle with 1½ cups (360 ml) cheddar cheese. Repeat layering.

- Top with last 3 noodles and reserved sauce.

- Cover and bake at 350° (176° C) for 45 minutes.

- Remove from oven and sprinkle remaining cheese on top.

- Return to oven uncovered and bake another 5 minutes or just until cheese melts. Let casserole stand 10 minutes before serving.

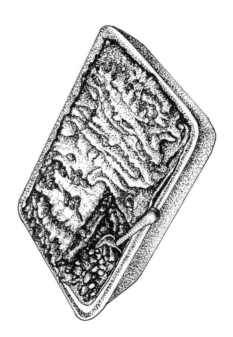

Chicken and Pasta

How could anything be easier?

4 chicken breast halves, cooked, cubed
2 (8 ounce) cartons sour cream   2 (227 g)
1 (7 ounce) box ready-cut spaghetti, uncooked   198 g
2 (10 ounce) cans cream of chicken soup   2 (280 g)
1 (4 ounce) can mushrooms, drained   114 g
½ cup (1 stick) butter, melted   120 ml
1 cup grated parmesan cheese   240 ml

- Combine chicken, sour cream, spaghetti, chicken soup, mushrooms, butter and ¼ teaspoon (1 ml) pepper in large bowl.

- Pour into greased 9 x 13-inch (23 x 33 cm) baking dish.

- Sprinkle cheese on top of casserole.

- Bake covered at 325° (162° C) for 50 minutes.

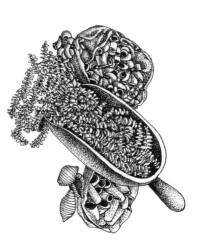

Creamed Chicken and Rice

4 cups cooked instant rice	1 L
6 tablespoons (¾ stick) butter, divided	90 ml
¼ cup flour	60 ml
2 cups milk	480 ml
2 teaspoons chicken bouillon granules	10 ml
1 teaspoon parsley flakes	5 ml
½ teaspoon celery salt	2 ml
4 cups cooked, cubed chicken	1 L
1 (16 ounce) box cubed processed cheese	.5 kg
1 (8 ounce) carton sour cream	227 g
1½ cups round, buttery cracker crumbs	360 ml

• Spread cooked rice into buttered 9 x 13-inch (23 x 33 cm) baking dish and set aside.

• In large saucepan melt 4 tablespoons (½ stick/60 ml) butter, stir in flour and mix until smooth. Gradually add milk, bouillon, seasonings and ½ teaspoon (2 ml) salt.

• Cook, stirring constantly, on medium heat for about 2 minutes or until sauce thickens.

• Reduce heat and add chicken, cheese and sour cream and stir until cheese melts.

• Spoon over rice in baking dish. Melt remaining 2 tablespoons (¼ stick/30 ml) butter and toss with cracker crumbs. Sprinkle over casserole.

• Bake uncovered at 325° (162° C) for 35 minutes or until hot.

Taco Casserole

2 (10 ounce) cans fiesta nacho cheese soup	2 (280 g)
½ cup milk	120 ml
1 (15 ounce) can whole kernel corn, drained	425 g
1 envelope taco seasoning	
1 sweet red bell pepper, chopped	
1 onion, chopped	
1 teaspoon ground cumin	5 ml
1 (12 ounce) package shredded cheddar-jack cheese	340 g
1 (13 ounce) package corn tostitos, slightly crushed	370 g
3-4 cups cooked, diced chicken breasts or turkey	
1 (4 ounce) can sliced black olives	1 L
	114 g

- Combine soup, milk, corn, taco seasoning, bell pepper, onion, cumin and ½ teaspoon (2 ml) salt in large bowl and mix well.

- In greased 9 x 13-inch (23 x 33 cm) baking dish, place 1 layer of half crushed tostitos, half chicken, half soup mixture and half cheese. Repeat layers ending with cheese on top.

- Bake covered at 325° (162° C) for 40 minutes or until casserole bubbles around edges.

- When ready to serve, sprinkle top of casserole with black olives.

Not JUST Chicken

This is a great recipe for leftover ham or turkey.

3 cups cooked, cubed chicken or turkey	710 ml
3 cups fully cooked cubed ham	710 ml
1 (8 ounce) package shredded cheddar cheese	227 g
1 (15 ounce) can English peas, drained	425 g
1 onion, chopped	
3 ribs celery, chopped	
1/4 cup (1/2 stick) butter	60 ml
1/3 cup plus 1 tablespoon flour	80ml;15ml
1 pint half-and-half cream	.5 kg
1/2 cup milk	120 ml
1 teaspoon dillweed	5 ml
Hot, cooked instant brown rice	
1/3 cup chopped walnuts	80 ml

• Combine chicken, ham, cheese and English peas in large bowl.

• In very large saucepan, saute onion and celery in butter until tender. Add flour and stir to make a paste.

• Gradually add cream, milk, dillweed and 1 teaspoon (5 ml) salt. Heat, stirring constantly, until mixture thickens.

• Add thickened cream mixture to chicken-ham mixture and mix well.

• Spoon into greased 2½-quart (2.5 L) baking dish. Use pretty baking dish for table.

• Cover and bake at 350° (176° C) for 20 minutes.

• Spoon chicken and ham casserole over hot brown rice.

Chicken-Ham Lasagna

1 (4 ounce) can chopped mushrooms, drained	114 g
1 large onion, chopped	
1/4 cup (1/2 stick) butter	60 ml
1/2 cup flour	120 ml
1/8 teaspoon ground nutmeg	.5 ml
1 (14 ounce) can chicken broth	396 g
1¾ cups half-and-half cream	420 ml
1 (3 ounce) package grated parmesan cheese	84 g
1 (16 ounce) package frozen broccoli florets, thawed	.5 kg
9 lasagna noodles, cooked, drained	
1½ cups cooked, finely diced ham, divided	360 ml
1 (12 ounce) package shredded Monterey Jack cheese, divided	340 g
2 cups cooked, shredded chicken breasts	480 ml

- Saute mushrooms and onion in butter in large skillet. While on medium heat, stir in flour, 1 teaspoon (5 ml) salt and ¼ teaspoon (1 ml) pepper and nutmeg and stir until they blend well. Gradually stir in broth and cream, cook and stir for about 2 minutes or until it thickens. Stir in parmesan cheese.

- Cut a few stems off broccoli and discard. Cut broccoli into smaller pieces. Add to cream mixture.

- Spread about ½ cup (120 ml) cream-broccoli mixture in greased 11 x 14-inch (30 x 36 cm) baking dish. Layer with three noodles, one-third of remaining broccoli mixture, ½ cup (120 ml) ham and 1 cup (240 ml) Monterey Jack cheese.

- Top with 3 more noodles, one-third of broccoli mixture, 1 cup (240 ml) ham and 1 cup (240 ml) Monterey Jack cheese. Pour in remaining noodles, ham and cream-broccoli mixture.

- Bake covered at 350° (176° C) for 50 minutes or until it bubbles. Sprinkle with remaining cheese. Let stand for 15 minutes before cutting into squares to serve.

Chinese Garden

This would be stretching a point to call this an authentic Chinese recipe, but this combination of ingredients makes a great tasting casserole. Try it, you'll like it!

1 (6 ounce) package fried rice with almonds and oriental seasoning	168 g
2 tablespoons butter	30 ml
1 onion, chopped	
2 cups celery, chopped	480 ml
1 (15 ounce) can Chinese vegetables, drained	425 g
1 (8 ounce) can sliced bamboo shoots	227 g
3½ cups cooked, chopped chicken	830 ml
1 (10 ounce) can cream of chicken soup	280 g
1 cup mayonnaise	240 ml
2 tablespoons soy sauce	30 ml
½ teaspoon garlic powder	2 ml
1 cup chop mein noodles	240 ml

- Cook rice according to package directions and set aside.

- Heat butter in large skillet and saute onion and celery. Add Chinese vegetables, bamboo shoots and chicken and mix well.

- In saucepan, heat chicken soup, mayonnaise, soy sauce, garlic powder and a little pepper just enough to mix well.

- In large bowl, combine rice, vegetable-chicken mixture and soup mixture and mix well.

- Transfer to greased 3-quart (3 L) baking dish. Sprinkle chow mein noodles over casserole.

- Bake uncovered at 350° (176° C) for 35 minutes.

Chicken, Veggies and Cashews

3½ cups cooked, cubed chicken breasts		830 ml
2 (10 ounce) cans cream of chicken soup		2 (280 g)
2 (15 ounce) cans chop suey vegetables, drained		2 (425 g)
1 (8 ounce) can sliced water chestnuts, drained		
¾ cup chopped cashew nuts		227 g
1 green bell pepper, chopped		180 ml
1 onion, chopped		
1 cup celery, chopped		240 ml
¼ teaspoon hot sauce		1 ml
¼ teaspoon curry powder		1 ml
1¼ cups chow mein noodles		300 ml

- Combine chicken, soup, vegetables, water chestnuts, cashew nuts, green pepper, onion, celery, hot sauce and curry powder in large bowl. Stir to mix well.

- Spoon into 9 x 13-inch (23 x 33 cm) baking dish sprayed with non-stick vegetable spray. Sprinkle chow mein noodles over top of casserole.

- Bale uncovered at 350° (176° C) for 35 minutes or until it bubbles at edges of casserole. Let set 5 minutes before serving.

Chicken Quesadillas

2 cups cooked, shredded chicken	480 ml
¾ cup salsa	180 ml
3 fresh green onions, chopped	
½ teaspoon ground cumin	2 ml
4 (8-inch) flour tortillas	4 (20 cm)
Butter, softened	
1 cup shredded Mexican 4-cheese blend	240 ml
Guacamole	

• Combine and cook chicken, salsa, onions, cumin and a little salt in skillet over medium high heat for about 5 minutes or just until it is hot.

• Brush 1 side of each tortilla with butter.

• Place half of chicken-mixture on 1 tortilla, other half on second tortilla.

• Sprinkle cheese equally over 2 tortillas and place other 2 tortillas, buttered side down, over cheese.

• Place on lightly greased baking sheet and bake at 400° (204° C) for about 10 minutes or until crisp. To serve cut into wedges. Serve with guacamole.

Baked Chicken Salad

4 cups cooked, chopped chicken breasts	1 L
¾ cup mayonnaise	180 ml
¼ cup onion, chopped	60 ml
1½ cups celery, chopped	360 ml
4 hard-boiled eggs, chopped	
1 (4 ounce) can chopped pimentos, drained	114 g
⅔ cup toasted almonds, chopped	160 ml
1 cup shredded cheddar cheese	240 ml
2 tablespoons lemon juice	30 ml
1 (10 ounce) can cream of chicken soup	280 g
1½ cups potato chips, crushed	360 ml

- Combine all ingredients and ½ teaspoon (2 ml) each of salt and pepper except crushed potato chips in large bowl. Spoon into buttered 9 x 13-inch (23 x 33 cm) baking dish.

- Cover and refrigerate for at least 8 hours. (Flavor improves when refrigerated overnight before cooking).

- When ready to bake, top casserole with crushed potato chips.

- Bake uncovered at 325° (162° C) for 35 to 40 minutes or until potato chips are light brown.

Turkey-Ham Tetrazzini

This is another old-fashioned dish modified to meet today's need for a "hurry-up meal" while retaining that nostalgic flavor.

1 (7 ounce) box thin spaghetti, cooked, drained	198 g
½ cup slivered almonds, toasted	120 ml
1 (10 ounce) can cream of mushroom soup	280 g
1 (10 ounce) can cream of chicken soup	280 g
¾ cup milk	180 ml
2 tablespoons dry white wine	30 ml
2½ cups diced, cooked, leftover turkey	600 ml
2 cups fully cooked, leftover diced ham	480 ml
½ cup green bell pepper, chopped	120 ml
½ cup red bell pepper, chopped	120 ml
½ cup halved pitted ripe olives	120 ml
1 (8 ounce) package shredded cheddar cheese	227 g

• Rinse cooked spaghetti with cold water to maintain firmness.

• Mix almonds, both soups, milk and wine in large bowl.

• Stir in spaghetti, turkey, ham, chopped peppers and pitted olives. Spoon into buttered 9 x 13-inch (23 x 33 cm) baking dish.

• Bake covered at 350° (176° C) for 35 minutes or until casserole is hot and bubbly.

• Remove cover and sprinkle top of casserole with cheese. Return to oven for 5 minutes.

Creamy Turkey Enchiladas

Forget about the calories. These enchiladas are worth it! Every time I make these I get raves.

2 tablespoons butter		30 ml
1 onion, finely chopped		
3 green onions, with tops, finely chopped		
½ teaspoon garlic powder		2 ml
1 (7 ounce) can chopped green chilies		198 g
2 (8 ounce) packages of cream cheese, softened		2 (227 g)
3 cups diced, cooked turkey or chicken		710 ml
8 (8-inch) flour tortillas		8 (20 cm)
2 (8 ounce) cartons whipping cream		2 (227 g)
1 (16 ounce) package shredded Mexican 4-cheese blend		.5 kg

- In large skillet, add butter and saute onions. Add garlic powder, green chilies and ½ teaspoon (2 ml) each of salt and pepper.

- Stir in cream cheese. Heat and stir just until cream cheese melts. Add diced turkey or chicken.

- Spread out 8 tortillas and spoon about 3 heaping tablespoons (45 ml) of turkey-cream cheese mixture on each tortilla. Use all turkey mixture. Roll tortillas and place seam-side down in lightly greased 11 x 15-inch (30 x 38 cm) baking dish. Pour whipping cream over enchiladas and sprinkle cheese over enchiladas.

- Bake uncovered at 350° (176° C) for 30 minutes or just until cream and cheese bubble but do not brown.

Tip: You need to use a long, wide spatula to serve these enchiladas. (Just in case you happen to have a couple enchiladas left over, heat them in the microwave and pour hot salsa over them. You'll love these leftovers).

Jazzy Turkey and Dressing

1 (6 ounce) package stuffing mix with seasoning packet	168 g
3 cups cooked, diced turkey	710 ml
1 (15 ounce) can golden hominy, drained	425 g
1 (7 ounce) can chopped green chilies, drained	198 g
½ cup red bell pepper, chopped	120 ml
2 tablespoons dried parsley flakes	30 ml
1 (10 ounce) can cream of chicken soup	280 g
1 (8 ounce) carton sour cream	227 g
2 tablespoons (¼ stick) butter, melted	30 ml
2 teaspoons ground cumin	10 ml
1 cup shredded mozzarella cheese	240 ml

- Combine all ingredients except cheese with ½ cup (120 ml) water in large mixing bowl. Mix well and pour into greased 9 x 13-inch (23 x 33 cm) baking dish.

- Bake covered at 350° (176° C) for 35 minutes.

- Uncover, sprinkle with cheese and return to oven.

- Bake additional 5 minutes or just until cheese melts.

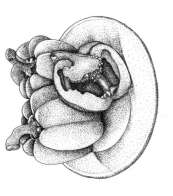

Tempting Chicken and Veggies

1½ pounds chicken breast tenderloins	680 g
3 tablespoons (⅓ stick) butter	45 ml
1 (6 ounce) box fried rice and seasoning packet	168 g
¼ cup sweet red bell pepper, chopped	60 ml
1 (10 ounce) package frozen broccoli spears, thawed	280 g
1 (10 ounce) package frozen corn, thawed	280 g

- Brown chicken tenderloins in butter in skillet. Remove chicken to large mixing bowl.

- In same skillet with remaining butter, saute rice until light brown and spoon into bowl with chicken.

- Add 2½ cups (600 ml) water, dash of pepper, bell pepper, broccoli spears and corn and mix well.

- Spoon into sprayed 9 x 13-inch (23 x 33 cm) baking dish.

- Cover and cook at 325° (162° C) for 25 minutes or until rice and vegetables are tender.

Beef

Beef and Noodles al Grande

This is an ideal casserole to make ahead of time for a quick and easy supper and it will serve about 14 people.

1½ -2 pounds lean ground beef	1 kg
1 onion, chopped	
1 green bell pepper, chopped	
1 (16 ounce) package cubed Mexican processed cheese	.5 kg
1 (10 ounce) can fiesta nacho cheese soup	280 g
1 (15 ounce) can stewed tomatoes	425 g
1 (10 ounce) can tomatoes and green chilies	280 g
1 (8 ounce) can whole kernel corn, drained	227 g
½ teaspoon chili powder	2 ml
¼ teaspoon ground mustard	1 ml
1 (8 ounce) package medium egg noodles	227 g
¼ cup (½ stick) butter, cut into 4-5 slices	60 ml
1 cup shredded cheddar cheese	240 ml

• Cook beef, onion and bell pepper in skillet until beef is no longer pink and vegetables are tender. Drain.

• Remove from heat, add processed cheese and stir until cheese melts.

• In large mixing bowl, combine fiesta nacho cheese, stewed tomatoes, tomatoes and green chilies, corn, chili powder, mustard and 1½ teaspoons (7 ml) salt and ½ teaspoon (2 ml) pepper. Add beef mixture and mix well.

• Cook egg noodles according to package directions and drain well. While noodles are still very hot, add butter and stir until it melts. Stir noodles in with tomato-beef mixture. Transfer to greased 10 x 14-inch (25 x 36 cm) baking dish.

• Cover and bake at 350° (176° C) for 45 minutes.

• Uncover and sprinkle cheese over casserole and return to oven for 4 to 10 minutes.

Zesty Rice and Beef

1 pound lean ground round steak	.5 kg
1 onion, chopped	
1 green bell pepper, chopped	
2½ cups cooked rice	600 ml
1 (15 ounce) whole kernel corn, drained	425 g
1 (15 ounce) can Mexican-style stewed	
tomatoes	425 g
1 (15 ounce) can diced tomatoes	425 g
2 teaspoons chili powder	10 ml
1 teaspoon garlic powder	5 ml
1 (8 ounce) package cubed processed cheese	227 g
1 cup buttery cracker crumbs	240 ml
½ cup chopped pecans or walnuts	120 ml
2 tablespoons butter, melted	30 ml

- Cook beef, onion and green pepper in large skillet or roaster over medium heat until beef is no longer pink. Drain well.

- Add rice, corn, stewed tomatoes, diced tomatoes, chili powder, garlic powder and 1 teaspoon (5 ml) salt and bring to boil. Remove from heat.

- Stir in processed cheese until it melts. Spoon into greased 9 x 13-inch (23 x 33 cm) baking dish.

- Combine cracker crumbs, pecans and melted butter. Sprinkle over top of casserole.

- Bake uncovered at 350° (176° C) for 25 minutes or until casserole is bubbly hot.

Stroganoff Casserole

1 (12 ounce) package medium egg noodles	340 g	
1½ pounds lean ground beef	680 g	
1 onion, chopped		
1 green bell pepper, seeded, chopped		
1 cup celery, chopped		
½ cup beef broth	240 ml	
	120 ml	
1 (6 ounce) can tomato paste	168 g	
1 (4 ounce) can sliced mushrooms, drained	114 g	
1 teaspoon dried oregano	5 ml	
½ teaspoon garlic powder	2 ml	
1 (8 ounce) carton sour cream	227 g	
1 (16 ounce) container small curd cottage cheese		
	227 g	
1 (8 ounce) package shredded mozzarella cheese	.5 kg	
1 cup shredded cheddar cheese	227 g	
	240 ml	

- Cook noodles according to package directions, drain and keep warm.

- In large skillet, cook ground beef until it crumbles and is no longer pink. Drain well.

- Stir in onion, bell pepper and celery. Cover and cook over medium-high heat for about 15 minutes, stirring occasionally. Stir in beef broth, tomato paste, mushrooms, oregano, garlic powder and ½ teaspoon (2 ml) salt and set aside.

- In large bowl combine sour cream and cottage cheese and mix well. Stir in cooked noodles and toss to coat.

- Spread half this mixture into buttered 9 x 13-inch (23 x 33 cm) baking dish. Top with half meat-vegetable mixture, half mozzarella cheese and half cheddar cheese. Repeat layers of remaining noodles and meat-vegetable mixture.

- Cover and bake at 350° (176° C) for about 25 minutes.

- Remove from oven and sprinkle with remaining cheeses. Bake uncovered for another 5 minutes.

Enchilada Casserole

1½ pounds lean ground beef	680 g
1 package taco seasoning mix	
8 flour or corn tortillas	
1 cup shredded cheddar cheese	240 ml
1 onion, chopped	
1 (10 ounce) can enchilada sauce	280 g
1 (7 ounce) can green chilies	198 g
1½ cups grated Monterey Jack cheese	360 ml
1 (8 ounce) carton sour cream	227 g

• Brown beef in skillet with salt and pepper until it crumbles and is no longer pink. Drain well.

• Add taco seasoning mix and 1¼ cups (300 ml) water to beef and simmer 5 minutes.

• In another skillet pour just enough oil to cover bottom of skillet and heat until oil is hot.

• Cook tortillas one at a time, until soft and limp, about 5 to 10 seconds on each side. Drain well on paper towels. As you are cooking tortillas, spoon ⅓ cup (80 ml) meat mixture into center of each tortilla.

• Sprinkle with small amount of cheddar cheese and 1 spoon full of chopped onion. Roll and place seam-side down in greased 9 x 13-inch (23 x 33 cm) baking dish.

• After filling all tortillas, add enchilada sauce and green chilies to remaining meat mixture. Spoon over tortillas.

• Cover and bake at 350° (176° C) for about 30 minutes.

• Uncover and sprinkle remaining cheddar cheese and Monterey Jack cheese over casserole.

• Return to oven just until cheese melts. Place dabs of sour cream over enchiladas to serve.

Enchilada Casserole Grande

1½ pounds lean ground beef	680 g
½ teaspoon minced garlic	2 ml
1 (8 ounce) package shredded colby-jack cheese blend	227 g
1 onion, chopped	
1 (10 ounce) can cream of chicken soup	280 g
1 (5 ounce) can evaporated milk	143 g
1 (8 ounce) box processed cheese, cubed	227 g
1 (.4 ounce) envelope ranch dip mix	14 g
1 (7 ounce) can chopped green chilies	198 g
1 (2 ounce) jar chopped pimento, drained	57 g
12 (8-inch) corn tortillas	12 (20 cm)

- Cook beef and garlic until beef crumbles and is no longer pink. Drain well.

- Stir in shredded colby-jack cheese and onion and set aside.

- In saucepan over medium heat, combine soup, evaporated milk and processed cheese and stir until cheese melts. Add dip mix, chilies and pimento.

- Pour water to depth of 1-inch (2.5 cm) in skillet and heat on high. (Keep heat on medium so water will stay hot.) Dip tortillas, 1 at a time, into hot water using tongs. Soak 2 to 3 seconds, remove and drain.

- Spoon about ⅓ cup (80 ml) meat mixture onto 1 side of each tortilla. Roll tightly and place seam-side down in greased 9 x 13-inch (23 x 33 cm) baking dish.

- Spoon cheese sauce over enchiladas.

- Bake covered at 350° (176° C) for 30 minutes.

- Uncover and bake another 10 minutes.

Meatball Veggies

1½ pounds lean ground beef	680 g
2 tablespoons ketchup	30 ml
1 egg	
⅓ cup seasoned bread crumbs	80 ml
1 (15 ounce) can whole kernel corn, drained	425 g
2 (10 ounce) cans diced tomatoes and green chilies	2 (280 g)
1 onion, chopped	
2 tablespoons cornstarch	30 ml
2 teaspoons Italian seasoning	10 ml
1 teaspoon minced garlic	5 ml
1 (28 ounce) package frozen hash brown potatoes, thawed	794 g
1 (8 ounce) package shredded cheddar cheese	227 g

• Combine beef, ketchup, egg, breadcrumbs and 1 teaspoon (5 ml) salt in mixing bowl.

• Shape into 1-inch (2.5 cm) balls and place in baking dish. Bake at 375° (190° C) for about 20 minutes

• In large saucepan, combine corn, tomatoes, green chilies, onion, ⅔ cup (160 ml) water, cornstarch, Italian seasoning and garlic. Cover and simmer for 10 minutes; add meatballs.

• Place hash browns in a greased 9 x 13-inch (23 x 33 cm) baking dish.

• Spoon meatball-tomato mixture over potatoes.

• Cover and bake at 350° (176° C) degrees for 45 minutes.

• Remove from oven, sprinkle cheese over top of casserole and return to oven for 10 minutes.

Beef

Just Say "Hot"

2 pounds lean ground beef		1 kg
1 onion, chopped		
1 green bell pepper, chopped		
1 tablespoon chili powder		15 ml
1 tablespoon ground cumin		15 ml
1 (15 ounce) can ranch-style beans, with liquid		425 g
1 (15 ounce) can whole kernel corn, drained		425 g
6 corn tortillas, cut into strips		
1 (8 ounce) package shredded cheddar cheese		227 g
1 (10 ounce) can diced tomatoes and green chilies		280 g
1 (10 ounce) can fiesta nacho cheese soup		280 g
1½ cups tortilla chips, crushed		360 ml

- Brown beef, onion and bell pepper in skillet and cook, stirring occasionally, for about 10 minutes. Drain well.

- Stir in chili powder, cumin and 1 teaspoon (5 ml) salt.

- Spoon meat mixture into greased 9 x 13-inch (23 x 33 cm) baking dish.

- Make layers of beans, corn, half tortilla strips and half cheese. Continue layers with remaining tortilla strips and remaining cheese.

- In saucepan, combine tomatoes and chilies with fiesta nacho cheese soup and heat just enough to mix well. Spoon this mixture over top of cheese.

- Cover and bake at 350° (176° C) for 20 minutes.

- Remove from oven and sprinkle crushed tortilla chips over top of casserole. Return to oven for another 20 minutes.

Beef

Chili Relleno Casserole

1 pound lean ground beef	.5 kg
1 bell pepper, chopped	
1 onion, chopped	
1 (4 ounce) can chopped green chilies	114 g
1 teaspoon oregano	5 ml
1 teaspoon dried cilantro leaves	5 ml
¾ teaspoon garlic powder	4 ml
2 (4 ounce) cans whole green chilies	2 (114 g)
1½ cups grated Monterey Jack cheese	360 ml
1½ cups grated sharp cheddar cheese	360 ml
3 large eggs	
1 tablespoon flour	15 ml
1 cup half-and-half cream	240 ml

• Brown meat with bell pepper and onion in skillet. Add chopped green chilies, oregano, cilantro, garlic powder and 1 teaspoon (5 ml) each of salt and pepper.

• Seed whole chilies and spread on bottom of greased 9 x 13-inch (23 x 33 cm) baking dish.

• Cover with meat mixture and sprinkle with cheeses.

• Combine eggs and flour and beat with fork until fluffy.

• Add half-and-half cream, mix and pour slowly over top of meat in casserole.

• Bake uncovered at 350° (176° C) for 35 minutes or until it browns lightly.

Chinese-Cashews Beef

This is good! It takes very little time to prepare and you will love serving it to your family or friends. A Chinese slaw goes great with it and it is easy to prepare. Everything can be made ahead of time.

1½ pounds lean ground beef		680 g
1 onion, chopped		
1 green bell pepper, chopped		
2 cups celery, chopped		
1 cup uncooked rice		240 ml
¼ cup soy sauce		60 ml
½ teaspoon hot sauce		2 ml
1 (15 ounce) can Chinese vegetables, drained		425 g
1 (4 ounce) can sliced mushrooms, drained		114 g
1¼ cups cashew nuts		300 ml
1 (10 ounce) can golden mushroom soup		280 g
½ teaspoon beef bouillon		7 ml
1½ cups chow mein noodles		360 ml

- Brown beef in skillet and stir well to break up meat.
- In large bowl, combine onion, bell pepper, celery, rice, soy sauce, hot sauce, Chinese vegetables, mushrooms, cashew nuts and ½ teaspoon (2 ml) salt.
- In saucepan, combine soup, 2 cups (480 ml) water and beef bouillon and heat just enough to mix well.
- Combine beef and soup mixture with onion-vegetable mixture.
- Pour into greased 9 x 13-inch (23 x 33 cm) baking dish. Cover and bake at 350° (176° C) for 50 minutes.
- Remove from oven and sprinkle noodles over casserole. Bake uncovered another 20 minutes.

Cabbage Rolls Along

1 large head cabbage, cored	
1½ pounds lean ground beef	680 g
1 egg, beaten	
3 tablespoons ketchup	45 ml
⅓ cup seasoned breadcrumbs	80 ml
2 tablespoons dried minced onion flakes	30 ml
2 (15 ounce) cans Italian stewed tomatoes	2 (425 g)
¼ cup cornstarch	60 ml
3 tablespoons brown sugar	45 ml
2 tablespoons Worcestershire sauce	30 ml

• Place cabbage in large kettle in boiling water for 10 minutes or until outer leaves are tender. Drain well. Rinse in cold water and remove 10 large outer leaves. Set aside.

• Take remaining cabbage and grate in slivers. Place in bottom of greased 9 x 13-inch (23 x 33 cm) baking dish.

• In large bowl combine ground beef, egg, ketchup, breadcrumbs and onion flakes and mix well.

• Place about ½ cup (120 ml) meat mixture on each cabbage leaf.

• Fold in sides and roll leaf to enclose filling.

• Place each rolled leaf over grated cabbage. Place stewed tomatoes in large saucepan.

• Combine cornstarch, brown sugar and Worcestershire sauce and spoon mixture into tomatoes. Cook on high heat, stirring constantly, until stewed tomatoes thicken. Pour over cabbage rolls.

• Cover and bake at 325° (162° C) for 1 hour.

Summer Cabbage Deluxe

1½ pounds lean ground beef	.7 kg
1 (16 ounce) package frozen broccoli florets, thawed	.5 kg
1 medium head cabbage, cored, coarsely chopped	
½ teaspoon sugar	2 ml
1 (8 ounce) carton sour cream	227 g
½ cup mayonnaise	120 ml
2 cups shredded white cheddar cheese	480 ml
1½ cups soft breadcrumbs	360 ml
2 tablespoons butter, melted	30 ml

• Cook beef in large skillet until meat is fairly browned.

• Lay broccoli florets out on a cutting board and cut off most of stems.

• Place broccoli florets, cabbage, 1 teaspoon (5 ml) salt, sugar and about ¾ cup (180 ml) water in large saucepan. Cook over medium heat about 10 minutes, stirring occasionally, only until vegetables are tender-crisp. Drain well.

• In large bowl, combine beef, broccoli-cabbage mixture, sour cream, mayonnaise, white cheddar cheese and 1 teaspoon (5 ml) salt and pepper. Transfer to buttered 3-quart (3 L) baking dish.

• Combine breadcrumbs and butter and sprinkle over casserole.

• Bake uncovered at 350° (176° C) for 25 minutes or until breadcrumbs are light brown.

Taco Pie

1½ pounds lean ground beef	680 g
½ green bell pepper, chopped	
1 teaspoon oil	5 ml
1 (15 ounce) can Mexican stewed tomatoes	425 g
1 tablespoon chili powder	15 ml
¼ teaspoon garlic powder	1 ml
1½ cups shredded cheddar cheese	360 ml
1 (6 ounce) package corn muffin mix	168 g
1 egg	
⅔ cup milk	160 ml

- Brown ground beef and bell pepper in large skillet in oil and drain well.

- Add ½ teaspoon (2 ml) salt, tomatoes, 1 cup (240 ml) water, chili powder and garlic powder. Cook on medium heat for about 10 minutes or until most of liquid is gone.

- Pour into greased 9 x 13-inch (23 x 33 cm) baking dish. Sprinkle cheese on top.

- Combine corn muffin mix, egg and milk and beat well. Pour over cheese.

- Bake at 375° (190° C) for 25 minutes or until corn muffin mix is light brown.

- Remove from oven and let set about 10 minutes before serving.

Enchilada Lasagna

1½ pounds lean ground beef	680 g
1 onion, chopped	
1 teaspoon minced garlic	5 ml
1 (15 ounce) can enchilada sauce	425 g
1 (15 ounce) can stewed tomatoes	425 g
1 teaspoon cumin	5 ml
1 egg	
1 (12 ounce) carton small curd cottage cheese	340 g
1 (12 ounce) package shredded 4-cheese blend, divided	340 g
8 (8-inch) corn tortillas, torn	8 (20 cm)
1 cup shredded cheddar cheese	240 ml

- Cook beef, onion and garlic in large skillet until meat is no longer pink.

- Stir in enchilada sauce, tomatoes, cumin and ½ teaspoon (5 ml) salt. Bring mixture to boil, reduce heat and simmer uncovered for 20 minutes.

- In small bowl, combine egg and cottage cheese.

- Spread one-third of meat sauce in greased 9 x 13-inch (23 x 33 cm) baking dish. Top with half of 4-cheese blend, tortillas and cottage cheese mixture. Repeat layers.

- Top with remaining meat sauce and sprinkle remaining cheddar cheese.

- Cover and bake at 325° (162° C) for 25 minutes. Uncover and bake 10 more minutes.

Italian Manicotti

1 pound lean ground beef	.5 kg
2 teaspoons minced garlic	10 ml
2 onions, chopped	
1 (28 ounce) can diced tomatoes, with juice	794 g
1 cup sliced fresh mushrooms	240 ml
2 teaspoons basil	10 ml
1 teaspoon Italian seasoning	5 ml
2 (10 ounce) boxes frozen spinach, thawed, well drained	
½ cup grated parmesan cheese	2 (280 g)
1 (16 ounce) carton small curd cottage cheese, drained	120 ml
¼ teaspoon ground nutmeg	.5 kg
14 manicotti shells, cooked al dente	1 ml

- Brown ground beef in large skillet, add garlic and onion and reduce heat to low. Simmer for 10 minutes and drain.

- Add tomatoes, mushrooms, basil, Italian seasoning and salt to taste; mix well. Bring to boil, reduce heat and simmer for 10 minutes, stir occasionally.

- Combine spinach, cottage cheese, and nutmeg.

- In sprayed 9 x 13-inch (23 x 33 cm) baking dish, spoon about one-third of beef sauce evenly over bottom of dish.

- Fill uncooked manicotti shells with spinach mixture and place on beef layer in baking dish. Repeat until manicotti shells are filled.

- Pour remaining beef sauce evenly over manicotti shells. Sprinkle parmesan cheese over top.

- Cover and bake at 325° (162° C) for 1½ hours.

Meatball Casserole

Yes, this is a crazy sounding recipe, but "wow" is it ever good! It is really rich and the family will love it!

1¼ pounds lean ground beef	567 g	
2 tablespoons ketchup	30 ml	
1 teaspoon Italian seasoning	5 ml	
1 egg		
2½ teaspoons minced garlic, divided	12 ml	
¼ cup seasoned breadcrumbs	60 ml	
¼ cup grated parmesan cheese	60 ml	
1 loaf Italian bread, cut into 1-inch (2.5 cm) slices		
1 (8 ounce) package cream cheese, softened	227 g	
½ cup mayonnaise	120 ml	
1 teaspoon Italian seasoning	5 ml	
1 (8 ounce) package shredded mozzarella cheese, divided	227 g	
1 (28 ounce) jar spaghetti sauce	794 g	

- Combine beef, ketchup, Italian seasoning, egg, 1 teaspoon (5 ml) minced garlic, breadcrumbs and parmesan cheese in large mixing bowl. Shape into small balls and place on rack in shallow baking pan.

- While meat cooks, arrange bread in single layer in ungreased 9 x 13-inch (23 x 33 cm) baking pan. (All of the bread might not be needed.)

- Bake at 375° (190° C) for 20 minutes or until they are no longer pink.

(Continued on next page.)

Beef

(Continued)

- In mixing bowl, beat cream cheese, mayonnaise, Italian seasoning and ½ teaspoon (2 ml) pepper and spread over bread slices. Sprinkle with 1 cup (240 ml) mozzarella.

- In bowl combine spaghetti sauce, ½ cup (120 ml) water, 1½ teaspoons (7 ml) minced garlic and ¾ teaspoon (4 ml) salt. Arrange meatballs over bread-cheese mixture and spoon spaghetti sauce over meatballs.

- Bake uncovered at 350° (176° C) for 25 minutes.

- Remove from oven and sprinkle remaining cheese over top of casserole. Return to oven for 10 minutes. Let casserole stand for about 10 minutes before serving.

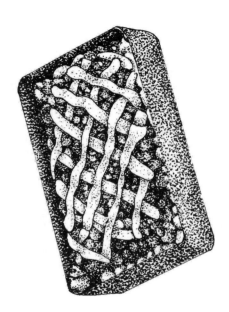

Italian Dinner

Baked Italian dishes are famous for their rich, flavorful sauces. This recipe tastes wonderful even as leftovers.

2 pounds ground round beef	1 kg
1 onion, chopped	
1 sweet red bell pepper, chopped	
2 ribs celery, chopped	
2 garlic cloves, finely minced	
1 (32 ounce) jar spaghetti sauce	1 kg
3 (6 ounce) jars sliced mushrooms, drained	3 (168 g)
½ teaspoon ground oregano	2 ml
1 teaspoon Italian seasoning	5 ml
1 (8 ounce) package medium egg noodles	227 g
1 (8 ounce) package cream cheese, softened	227 g
1 pint carton sour cream	.5 kg
1 cup grated parmesan cheese	240 ml
1 (16 ounce) package shredded mozzarella cheese	.5 kg

- Brown beef, onion, bell pepper, celery and garlic in very large skillet and drain well.

- Add spaghetti sauce, mushrooms, oregano, Italian seasonings and dash of salt and pepper. Heat to boiling, turn heat down and simmer for about 15 minutes.

- Cook noodles according to package directions and drain.

- With electric mixer, beat cream cheese until creamy and add sour cream and cheeses.

- Butter deep 11 x 14-inch (30 x 36 cm) baking dish. Layer half noodles, half beef mixture and half cheeses. Repeat layers.

- Bake covered at 325° (162° C) for 30 minutes. Remove covering and bake another 10 to 15 minutes.

Beef

Simple Spaghetti Bake

8 ounces spaghetti	227 g
1 pound lean ground beef	.5 kg
1 green bell pepper, finely chopped	
1 onion, chopped	
1 (10 ounce) can tomato bisque soup	280 g
1 (15 ounce) can tomato sauce	425 g
2 teaspoons Italian seasoning	10 ml
1 (8 ounce) can whole kernel corn, drained	227 g
1 (4 ounce) can black sliced olives, drained	114 g
1 (12 ounce) package shredded	
cheddar cheese	340 g

• Cook spaghetti according to package directions, drain and set aside.

• In skillet, cook beef, bell pepper and onion and drain.

• Add remaining ingredients, ⅓ cup (80 ml) water and ½ teaspoon (2 ml) salt and spaghetti to beef mixture and stir well. Pour into greased 9 x 13-inch (23 x 33 cm) baking dish and cover.

• Refrigerate 2 to 3 hours.

• Bake covered at 350° (176° C) for 45 minutes.

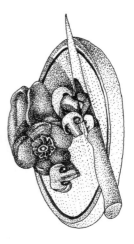

Casserole Beef Stew

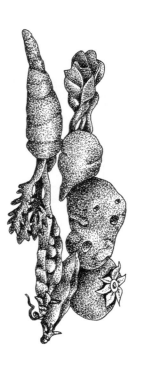

1 (2-3 pounds) chuck roast, cut in bite-size pieces	1.3 kg
2 tablespoons oil	30 ml
1 cup carrots, sliced	240 ml
2 onions, chopped	
4 potatoes, peeled, cubed	
1 cup celery, chopped	240 ml
1 (10 ounce) can golden cream of mushroom soup	280 g
½ cup burgundy wine	120 ml

- In large skillet brown pieces of roast in oil.

- Place in large sprayed roasting pan.

- Add all remaining ingredients with 2 teaspoons (10 ml) salt, 1 teaspoon (5 ml) pepper and ½ cup (120 ml) water.

- Cover and bake at 300° (148° C) for 5 hours.

Company Beef and Pasta

2 pounds lean, ground beef	1 kg
2 onions, chopped	
1 green bell pepper, chopped	
¾ teaspoon garlic powder	4 ml
1 (14 ounce) jar spaghetti sauce	396 g
1 (15 ounce) can Italian stewed tomatoes	425 g
1 (4 ounce) can sliced mushrooms, drained	114 g
1 (8 ounce) package rotini pasta, divided	227 g
1½ pints sour cream, divided	680 g
1 (8 ounce) package sliced provolone cheese	227 g
1 (8 ounce) package shredded mozzarella cheese	227 g

• Brown and cook beef in deep skillet or kettle and stir often to break up pieces. Drain off excess fat.

• Add onions, bell pepper, garlic powder, spaghetti sauce, stewed tomatoes and mushrooms and mix well. Simmer 20 minutes.

• Cook rotini according to package directions and drain. Pour half rotini into buttered deep 11 x 14-inch (30 x 36 cm) baking dish.

• Cover with half meat-tomato mixture and half sour cream. Top with slices of provolone cheese. Repeat process once more ending with mozzarella cheese.

• Cover and bake at 325° (162° C) for 35 minutes.

• Remove cover and continue baking another 10 to 15 minutes or until mozzarella cheese melts.

Fettuccine Italian

6 ounces fettuccini, cooked	168 g
½ pound lean ground beef	227 g
1 teaspoon minced garlic	5 ml
1 onion, minced	
1 (8 ounce) can tomato sauce	227 g
1 (15 ounce) can Italian stewed tomatoes, with juice	425 g
1 teaspoon Italian seasoning	5 ml
2 eggs, divided	
1 (8 ounce) package shredded mozzarella cheese	227 g
1 cup small curd cottage cheese	240 ml
1 (3 ounce) package grated parmesan cheese	84 g

• In large skillet, brown beef and stir to crumble. Add garlic and onion; cook 5 minutes.

• Add tomato sauce, stewed tomatoes and Italian seasoning. Stir and bring to boil. Reduce heat, cover and simmer for 10 to 12 minutes, stirring occasionally.

• Beat 1 egg and stir in fettuccine and mozzarella cheese.

• Spoon mixture into ungreased, deep 10-inch (25 cm) pie plate and press down on bottom and sides of plate to pack fettuccine mixture.

• Mix remaining egg and cottage cheese in separate bowl. Spoon over fettuccine in pie plate and smooth over surface.

• Spoon beef mixture evenly over top. Sprinkle parmesan evenly over top.

• Bake uncovered at 350° (176° C) for 30 minutes.

Cheesy Stuffed Bell Peppers

6 green bell peppers
1½ pounds lean ground beef   680 g
½ cup onion, chopped   120 ml
¾ cup cooked rice   180 ml
1 egg
2 (15 ounce) cans Italian stewed
  tomatoes, divided   2 (425 g)
½ teaspoon garlic powder   2 ml
1 tablespoon Worcestershire sauce   15 ml
1 (8 ounce) package shredded cheddar
  cheese, divided   227 g

- Cut off small portion of tops of bell pepper and remove seeds and membranes. Place in roasting pan with salted water and boil. Cook 10 minutes so they will be only partially done. Drain and set aside to cool.

- Brown ground beef and onion in skillet and drain. Add rice, egg, 1 can tomatoes, Worcestershire, garlic and 1 teaspoon (5 ml) each of salt and pepper. Simmer 5 minutes. Remove from heat, add 1 cup (240 ml) cheese and mix well.

- Stuff peppers with mixture and set upright in buttered, round baking dish. (You may have to trim little slivers off bottoms of peppers so they will sit upright.)

- Pour remaining can of tomatoes over top and around peppers.

- Bake uncovered at 350° (176° C) for 25 minutes.

- Remove from oven and sprinkle remaining cheese on top and return to oven for 10 minutes.

Easy Winter Warmer

This is such a good spaghetti sauce on noodles and

is a great substitute for cream sauce.

1 (12 ounce) package medium egg noodles		340 g
3 tablespoons butter		45 ml
1½ pounds lean ground round beef		680 g
1 (10 ounce) package frozen seasoning blend (chopped onions and peppers), thawed		280 g
1 (28 ounce) jar spaghetti sauce		794 g
1 (12 ounce) package shredded mozzarella cheese		340 g

• Cook noodles according to package directions in pot of boiling water with a dab of oil and salt. Drain thoroughly, add butter and stir until butter melts.

• Brown beef and onions and peppers and drain thoroughly.

• Pour half of spaghetti sauce in bottom of buttered 9 x 13-inch (23 x 33 cm) baking dish.

• Layer half noodles, half beef and half cheese. Repeat for second layer.

• Bake covered at 350° (176° C) for about 30 minutes or until dish is hot.

Super Spaghetti Pie

*This is a great recipe to make ahead of time and have ready for a
late supper after the game or a midnight supper when teen-agers
demand "food"! What better than "food" that resembles pizza?*

6 ounces spaghetti	168 g
⅓ cup grated parmesan cheese	80 ml
1 egg, beaten	
1 tablespoon butter, melted	15 ml
1 cup small curd cottage cheese, drained	240 ml
½ pound lean ground beef	227 g
½ pound sausage	227 g
½ cup onion, chopped	120 ml
1 (15 ounce) can tomato sauce	425 g
1 teaspoon garlic powder	5 ml
1 tablespoon sugar	15 ml
1 teaspoon oregano	5 ml
½ cup shredded mozzarella cheese	120 ml

- Cook spaghetti according to package directions.
  While spaghetti is still warm, stir in parmesan cheese,
  egg and butter in large bowl.

- Pour into well greased 10-inch (25 cm) pie plate and
  pat mixture down on sides and bottom to form crust.

- Spoon cottage cheese over spaghetti crust.

- In skillet brown ground meat, sausage and onion.
  Drain fat and add tomato sauce and seasonings.
  Simmer 10 minutes and stir occasionally.

- Spoon meat mixture over cottage cheese.

- Bake at 350° (176° C) for 30 minutes.

- Arrange mozzarella on top and return to oven just
  until cheese melts.

Pepper Steak

You can't beat this tender sirloin and colorful peppers with a tasty beef sauce.

1½ pounds boneless sirloin, ¾-inch (1.8 cm) thick	680 g	
3 tablespoons oil	45 ml	
1 green and 1 red bell pepper, thinly sliced		
1 onion, cut in wedges		
1 teaspoon minced garlic	5 ml	
1 (14 ounce) can beef broth	396 g	
2 tablespoons cornstarch	30 ml	
1 (10 ounce) can beefy mushroom soup	280 g	
2 tablespoons soy sauce	30 ml	
½ teaspoon ground ginger	2 ml	
4 cups hot cooked, white rice	1 L	

- Slice beef across grain into thin strips. Pour oil in large skillet and brown steak on high heat. Reduce heat and cook on low for 10 minutes.

- With slotted spoon, place beef in 3-quart (3 L) baking dish.

- Saute bell peppers, onion and garlic in skillet with remaining oil. Combine beef broth and cornstarch and mix well.

- Stir in beef broth, soup, soy sauce, ginger and ½ teaspoon (2 ml) salt and heat to boiling.

- Pour soup mixture over beef, cover and bake at 350° (176° C) for about 65 minutes. Serve over hot rice.

Round Steak Casserole

This is definitely not a luncheon dish. The men are going to call for this "beef" over and over again.

2 pounds lean round steak, tenderized	1 kg
3 tablespoons oil	45 ml
1 onion, chopped	
1 cup uncooked rice	240 ml
1 (14 ounce) can beef broth	396 g
1 tablespoon dried parsley flakes	15 ml
1/2 teaspoon garlic powder	2 ml
2 tablespoons Worcestershire sauce	30 ml
1 green and 1 red bell pepper, sliced	

• Trim fat from steak and cut into serving-size pieces. Season with a little salt and pepper.

• Pour oil in large skillet and brown steak on both sides. Remove to greased 9 x 13-inch (23 x 33 cm) baking dish.

• In bowl, combine onion, rice, beef broth, 1 soup can plus 1/3 cup (80 ml) water, parsley flakes, garlic powder, a little salt, Worcestershire and bell peppers. Spoon over steak.

• Cover and bake at 350° (176° C) for 45 minutes.

Flank Steak Royal

2 (1½ pounds each) beef flank steaks	2 (680 g)	
1 (6 ounce) jar marinated artichoke hearts, drained, chopped	168 g	
2 bunches fresh green onions, with tops, finely chopped		
1 pound bacon, fried, drained, crumbled	.5 kg	
1½ cups soft breadcrumbs	360 ml	
1½ cups grated romano cheese	360 ml	
2 cups fresh spinach, very finely chopped	480 ml	
2 teaspoons minced garlic Worcestershire sauce		
½ cup (1 stick) butter	10 ml	
½ pound fresh mushrooms, sliced	120 ml	
1 onion, sliced	227 g	
2 tablespoons dried parsley	30 ml	
2 (14 ounce) cans beef broth	2 (396 g)	
2 cups instant brown rice, cooked	480 ml	

- Tenderize flank steaks twice or ask butcher to tenderize.

- In large bowl, combine artichoke hearts, onions, crispy bacon, breadcrumbs, romano cheese and very finely chopped fresh spinach and toss thoroughly.

- Divide mixture in half and pat evenly over flank steaks. Carefully roll each steak in jelly-roll fashion. With cotton twine, tie securely in 6 to 8 places and seal ends securely.

- Rub steak with Worcestershire sauce and minced garlic.

(Continued on next page.)

Beef

(*Continued*)

- Drop butter in large skillet on medium low heat and sear meat on all sides until brown. Place in large roasting pan.

- In medium bowl, mix sliced mushrooms, chopped onion, parsley and beef broth and mix well.

- Pour over steak rolls, cover and cook at 325° (162° C) for 1 hour or until fork tender.

- Remove cover and cook another 10 minutes for steak to brown slightly. Remove from pan and allow to stand for about 10 minutes before slicing in about ¾-inch (1.8 cm) slices.

- Arrange rice on large platter and place sliced steak over rice. Use remaining broth as a sauce to serve with steak and rice.

Best Pot Roast Dinner

Well, we can't really say this is a casserole, but if you stretch your imagination, it is because you have your whole meal cooked in one container and everybody loves pot roast.

4 pound boneless rump roast	1.8 kg
Garlic powder	
6 potatoes, peeled, quartered	
8 carrots, peeled, quartered	
3 onions, peeled, quartered	
3 tablespoons cornstarch	45 ml

• Set roast in roasting pan with lid and sprinkle liberally with salt, pepper and garlic powder. Add 1½ cups (360 ml) water and cook covered at 375° (190° C) for about 30 minutes.

• Turn heat down to 325° (162° C) and cook for about 2½ to 3 hours or until roast is fork tender.

• Add potatoes, carrots and onions. Cook another 35 to 40 minutes.

• Lift roast out of roaster and place on serving platter.

• Place potatoes, carrots and onions around roast.

• Combine cornstarch and ¾ cup (180 ml) water and add to juices left in roaster. Add ½ teaspoon (2 ml) each of salt and pepper and stir to make gravy.

• Cook on high on top of stove until gravy thickens, stirring constantly. Serve in gravy boat with roast and vegetables.

Ravioli and More

1 pound lean ground beef	.5 kg
1 teaspoon garlic powder	5 ml
1 large onion, chopped	
2 zucchini squash, grated	
¼ cup (½ stick) butter	60 ml
1 (28 ounce) jar spaghetti sauce	794 g
1 (25 ounce) package ravioli with portobello mushrooms, cooked	708 g
1 (12 ounce) package shredded mozzarella cheese	340 g

• Brown ground beef in large skillet until no longer pink and drain. Add garlic powder and ½ teaspoon (2 ml) each of salt and pepper.

• In saucepan cook onion and zucchini in butter just until tender-crisp and stir in spaghetti sauce.

• In buttered 9 x 13-inch (23 x 33 cm) baking dish, spread ½ cup (120 ml) sauce. Layer half of ravioli, half spaghetti sauce, half beef and half cheese.

• Repeat layers, but omit remaining cheese. Cover and bake at 350° (176° C) for 35 minutes.

• Uncover and sprinkle remaining cheese. Let stand 10 minutes before serving.

Sombrero Olé

1 (1½ pounds) package lean ground beef	680 g	
1 large onion, chopped		
1 red and 1 yellow bell pepper, chopped		
3 cups zucchini, chopped	710 ml	
1 envelope taco seasoning		
1 cup uncooked rice	240 ml	
1 (16 ounce) jar chunky salsa	.5 kg	
1½ cups grated cheddar cheese	360 ml	
2 cups tortilla chips, lightly crushed	480 ml	

• Brown ground beef in large skillet, drain and add 1 teaspoon (5 ml) salt.

• Add onion, bell peppers, zucchini, ½ cup (120 ml) water and taco seasoning. Stir and saute until vegetables are tender.

• In separate saucepan, cook rice according to package directions.

• In sprayed 9 x 13-inch (23 x 33 cm) baking dish, spoon rice over bottom of dish and layer beef mixture, salsa and cheese.

• Bake at 350° (176° C) for 20 to 25 minutes.

• Remove from oven and sprinkle tortilla chips over top. Bake for another 10 minutes.

Pork

Pork Chop-Cheddar Bake

8 boneless pork chops

1 (10 ounce) can cream of mushroom soup	280 g
1 cup uncooked rice	240 ml
1½ cups grated cheddar cheese, divided	360 ml
½ cup minced onion	120 ml
⅓ cup bell pepper, chopped	80 ml
1 (4 ounce) can sliced mushrooms, drained	114 g
1 (6 ounce) can french-fried onions	168 g

• In large skillet, brown pork chops lightly. Drain and place in greased 9 x 13-inch (23 x 33 cm) baking dish.

• In same skillet, combine soup, 1¼ cups (300 ml) water, rice, ½ cup (120 ml) cheese, onion, bell pepper and mushrooms and mix well. Pour over pork chops.

• Cover with foil and bake at 325° (162° C) for 1 hour 10 minutes.

• Uncover and top with remaining cheese and french-fried onions. Return to oven just until cheese melts.

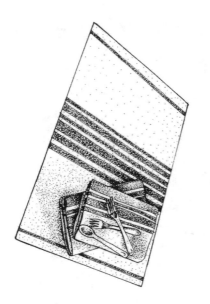

Apricot-Pork Chops

1 (15 ounce) can apricot halves, with juice	425 g
8 (½-inch) thick boneless pork chops	8 (1.2 cm)
3 tablespoons butter	45 ml
⅓ cup celery, chopped	80 ml
1 yellow bell pepper, chopped	
2½ cups uncooked instant rice	600 ml
1 teaspoon chicken bouillon	5 ml
⅓ cup golden raisins	80 ml
½ teaspoon ground ginger	2 ml
½ cup slivered almonds	120 ml

• Place apricots in food processor, cover and process until smooth. Set aside.

• In skillet, brown pork chops on both sides in butter, reduce heat and simmer for about 10 minutes. Remove pork chops to heated plate.

• In same skillet, saute celery and bell pepper and add rice, ¾ cup (180 ml) water, bouillon, raisins, ginger, ½ teaspoon (2 ml) salt and apricot puree and bring to boil.

• Remove from heat and stir in almonds. Spoon into 9 x 13-inch (23 x 33 cm) baking dish.

• Place pork chops on top of rice mixture.

• Cover and bake at 350° (176°) for 20 minutes.

Pork Chops and Apples

6 (¾-inch) bone-in pork chops	6 (1.8 cm)
¼ cup (½ stick) butter, divided	60 ml
6 cups stuffing croutons	1.5 L
1 cup green apples, peeled, chopped	240 ml
½ cup celery, chopped	120 ml
½ cup golden raisins	120 ml
½ cup chopped pecans	120 ml
2 teaspoons rubbed sage	10 ml
1 tablespoon dijon-style mustard	15 ml

- Brown pork chops on both sides in 2 tablespoons (30 ml) butter in large skillet and set aside.

- In same skillet, melt remaining butter, stir in croutons, chopped apples, celery, raisins, pecans, ½ cup (120 ml) water, sage and 1 teaspoon (5 ml) salt and mix well.

- Place crouton mixture into greased 7 x 11-inch (18 x 28 cm) baking dish. Top with pork chops.

- Spread thin layer of mustard over each pork chop. Cover and bake at 325° (162° C) for 40 minutes.

- Uncover and bake another 10 minutes.

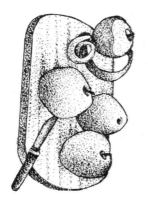

Pork Chop Casserole

6 (¾-inch) boneless pork chops	6 (1.8 cm)
1 green bell pepper	
1 yellow bell pepper, seeded, chopped	
1 (15 ounce) can tomato sauce	425 g
1 (15 ounce) can Italian stewed tomatoes, with juice	425 g
1 teaspoon minced garlic	5 ml
1½ cups uncooked long grain rice	360 ml

• Sprinkle pork chops with ½ teaspoon (2 ml) each of salt and pepper. In skillet, brown pork chops in a little oil. Remove chops from skillet and set aside.

• Cut top off green pepper, remove seeds and cut 6 rings from green bell pepper and set aside.

• In separate bowl, combine chopped yellow pepper, tomato sauce, Italian stewed tomatoes, 1 cup (240 ml) water, garlic and ½ teaspoon (2 ml) salt and stir well.

• Spread rice in greased 9 x 13-inch (23 x 33 cm) baking dish and slowly pour tomato mixture over rice.

• Arrange pork chops over rice and place pepper ring over each chop.

• Cover and bake at 350° (176° C) for 1 hour or until chops and rice are tender.

Orange Pork Chops

6 (½-inch) boneless pork chops	6 (1.2 cm)	
2 tablespoons oil	30 ml	
1⅓ cups uncooked instant rice	320 ml	
1 cup orange juice	240 ml	
¼ teaspoon ground ginger	1 ml	
1 (10 ounce) can condensed chicken with rice soup	280 g	
½ cup chopped walnuts	120 ml	

- Sprinkle a little salt and pepper over pork chops and brown in skillet with oil.

- Sprinkle rice into greased 7 x 11-inch (18 x 28 cm) baking dish. Add orange juice and arrange pork chops over rice.

- Add ginger to soup and stir right in can. Pour soup over pork chops.

- Sprinkle walnuts over tops of pork chops.

- Cover and bake at 350° (176° C) for 25 minutes.

- Uncover and bake 10 minutes longer or until rice is tender.

Italian-Style Pork Chops

6 (³/₄-inch) thick bone-in pork chops	6 (1.8 cm)
2 green bell peppers	
1 (15 ounce) can tomato sauce	425 g
1 (15 ounce) can Italian-style stewed tomatoes, with juice	425 g
½ onion, chopped	
1 teaspoon Italian seasoning	5 ml
1 clove garlic, minced	
1 tablespoon Worcestershire sauce	15 ml
½ cup uncooked brown rice	120 ml

• Sprinkle pork chops with a little salt and pepper. In skillet, brown chops on both sides in a little oil. Remove chops from skillet, drain and set aside.

• Cut top off 1 bell pepper and remove seeds. Cut 6 (¼-inch/.6 cm) thick rings from 1 bell pepper and set aside. Seed and chop remaining bell pepper.

• Combine chopped bell pepper, tomato sauce, stewed tomatoes, 1 cup (240 ml) water, onion, Italian seasoning, garlic, Worcestershire and ½ teaspoon (2 ml) each of salt and pepper and mix well.

• Spread rice evenly in lightly greased 9 x 13-inch (23 x 33 cm) baking pan. Slowly pour tomato mixture over rice.

• Arrange pork chops over rice mixture and top each pork chop with pepper ring.

• Bake covered at 350° (176° C) for 1 hour or until rice is tender.

Pepperoni Twirls

2 cups tomato-spinach macaroni twirls	480 ml
1 pound bulk Italian sausage	.5 kg
1 onion, chopped	
1 green bell pepper, chopped	
1 (15 ounce) can pizza sauce	425 g
1 (8 ounce) can tomato sauce	227 g
⅓ cup milk	80 ml
1 (3 ounce) package sliced pepperoni, halved	
1 (4 ounce) jar sliced mushrooms, drained	84 g
1 (2 ounce) can sliced ripe olives, drained	57 g
1 (8 ounce) package shredded mozzarella cheese, divided	227 g

- Cook macaroni twirls according to package directions and drain.

- In skillet over medium heat, cook sausage, onion and bell pepper until sausage is no longer pink and drain.

- In large bowl, combine pizza sauce, tomato sauce and milk. Stir in sausage mixture, macaroni twirls, pepperoni, mushrooms, olives and half cheese and mix well.

- Spoon into greased 9 x 13-inch (23 x 33 cm) baking dish. Cover and bake at 350° (176° C) for 30 minutes.

- Remove from oven and sprinkle remaining cheese over top of casserole and return to oven for 5 to 10 minutes or just until cheese is melted.

Zesty Ziti

1 pound Italian sausage links, cut into	
½-inch pieces/1.2 cm	.5 kg
1 onion, coarsely chopped	
1 green bell pepper, sliced	
1 (15 ounce) can diced tomatoes	425 g
1 (15 ounce) can Italian stewed tomatoes	425 g
2 tablespoons ketchup	30 ml
1 (16 ounce) package ziti pasta	.5 kg
1 cup shredded mozzarella cheese	240 ml

• Cook sausage, onion and bell pepper in a little oil over medium heat in large skillet and drain.

• Add diced tomatoes, stewed tomatoes and ketchup and mix well.

• Cook ziti according to package directions and drain.

• In large bowl, combine sausage-tomato mixture and toss with pasta and cheese.

• Spoon into greased 3-quart (3 L) baking dish. Cover and bake at 350° (176° C) from 20 minutes.

Pork-Stuffed Eggplant

1 large eggplant	
¾ pound ground pork	340 g
½ pound pork sausage	227 g
1 egg	
½ cup dry breadcrumbs	120 ml
½ cup grated romano cheese	120 ml
1 tablespoon dried parsley flakes	15 ml
1 tablespoon dried onion flakes	15 ml
1 teaspoon dried oregano	5 ml
1 (15 ounce) can stewed tomatoes	425 g
1 (8 ounce) can tomato sauce	227 g

- Cut off eggplant stem and cut eggplant in half lengthwise. Scoop out and reserve center, leaving ½-inch (1.2 cm) shell.

- Steam shell halves for about 5 minutes or just until tender. Drain well.

- Cube reserved eggplant and cook in saucepan with boiling salted water for about 6 minutes, drain well and set aside.

- In skillet over medium heat, cook pork and sausage until no longer pink and drain.

- Add eggplant cubes, egg, breadcrumbs, cheese, parsley flakes, onion flakes, oregano, and ½ teaspoon (2 ml) each of salt and pepper and mix well.

- Fill shells and place in greased 7 x 11-inch (18 x 28 cm) baking dish. Pour stewed tomatoes and tomato sauce over eggplant.

- Cover and bake at 350° (176° C) for 30 minutes.

Pork Loin with Fruit Sauce

1 (4 pound) pork loin roast	1.8 kg
1 teaspoon dried rosemary	5 ml
2 tablespoons (¼ stick) butter	30 ml
1 cup orange juice	240 ml
1 (16 ounce) can whole berry cranberry sauce	.5 kg
1 cup apricot preserves	240 ml
1 (14 ounce) can chicken broth	396 g
1 teaspoon red wine vinegar	5 ml
1 teaspoon sugar	5 ml
1 tablespoon white wine	
Worcestershire sauce	15 ml
Cooked white rice	

- Place roast in shallow roasting pan. Sprinkle with rosemary and 1 teaspoon (5 ml) pepper.

- Bake uncovered at 350° (176° C) for 1 hour.

- In large saucepan, combine remaining ingredients and 1 teaspoon (5 ml) salt. Bring ingredients to boiling point, reduce heat and simmer for 20 minutes.

- Remove roast from oven and spoon about 1 cup (240 ml) sauce over roast. Return to oven and cook additional hour or until meat thermometer reads 165° (74° C). Let roast stand several minutes before slicing.

- Spoon meat juices from roast into fruit sauce. Heat and serve with pork roast. Serve over hot cooked rice.

Fiesta Pork Casserole

*This zesty casserole is so easy to put together and it really
gets your attention! It is specially nice for a change of pace
from the usual Mexican dish with ground beef.*

2 pounds boneless pork tenderloin	1 kg	
1 onion, chopped		
1 green bell pepper, chopped		
3 tablespoons oil	45 ml	
1 (15 ounce) can black beans, rinsed, drained	425 g	
1 (10 ounce) can fiesta nacho cheese	280 g	
1 (15 ounce) can stewed tomatoes	425 g	
1 (4 ounce) can chopped green chilies	114 g	
1 cup instant brown rice, cooked	240 ml	
3/4 cup salsa	180 ml	
2 teaspoons ground cumin	10 ml	
1/2 teaspoon garlic powder	2 ml	
3/4 cup shredded Mexican 3-cheese blend	180 ml	

- Cut pork into 1-inch (2.5 cm) cubes. In very large skillet or roasting pan, brown and cook pork, onion and bell pepper in oil until pork is no longer pink. Drain.

- Add beans, nacho cheese soup, stewed tomatoes, green chilies, rice, salsa, cumin, 1/2 teaspoon (2 ml) salt and garlic powder. Cook on medium heat, stirring occasionally, until mixture bubbles.

- Spoon into buttered 4-quart (4 L) baking dish. Bake uncovered at 350° (176° C) for 30 minutes or until it bubbles around edges.

- Remove from oven and sprinkle with cheese. Let stand a few minutes before serving.

One-Dish Pork and Peas

So many of our casseroles are chicken, but pork is so good and always tender. This blend of ingredients makes a delicious dish.

1-1½ pounds pork tenderloin, cut into ½-inch (1.2 cm) cubes	680 g	
1 cup celery, sliced	240 ml	
1 onion, chopped		
1 sweet red bell pepper, chopped		
1 (8 ounce) package small egg noodles, cooked, drained	227 g	
1 (10 ounce) can cream of chicken soup	280 g	
½ cup half-and-half cream	120 ml	
1 (10 ounce) package frozen green peas, thawed	280 g	
1 cup seasoned dry breadcrumbs	240 ml	
⅓ cup chopped walnuts	80 ml	

• Brown cubed pork in large skillet in a little oil. Reduce heat and cook for about 20 minutes. Remove pork to separate dish.

• In little oil saute celery, onion and bell pepper.

• Add pork, noodles, soup, cream, peas and ½ teaspoon (2 ml) each of salt and pepper.

• Spoon into buttered 3-quart (3 L) baking dish. Sprinkle with breadcrumbs and walnuts.

• Bake uncovered at 350° (176° C) for about 25 minutes or until bubbly.

Peppered-Tenderloin

1 pork tenderloin, thinly sliced

Olive oil
1 red and 1 green bell pepper, thinly sliced
½ pound fresh mushrooms, quartered   227 g
1 onion, coarsely chopped
1 teaspoon minced garlic   5 ml
½ cup beef broth   120 ml
2 tablespoons ketchup   30 ml
1 teaspoon lemon juice   5 ml
1 teaspoon dried tarragon   5 ml
1 tablespoon flour   15 ml
½ cup sour cream   120 ml
Cooked noodles

- In large skillet, brown pork slices in a little olive oil. Remove and keep warm.

- In same skillet, saute peppers, mushrooms, onion and garlic in a little more oil.

- Add broth, ketchup, lemon juice, tarragon and ½ teaspoon (2 ml) pepper. Simmer uncovered for 3 minutes. Return pork to skillet.

- Combine flour with sour cream and stir into pork mixture. Spoon into greased 7 x 11-inch (18 x 28 cm) baking dish.

- Cover and cook at 325° (162° C) for 20 minutes. Serve over hot cooked noodles.

Pork-Noodles Supreme

2 pounds pork tenderloin, cut into 1-inch
  (2.5 cm) cubes   1 kg
2 ribs celery, chopped
1 red and 1 green bell pepper, chopped
1 onion, chopped
1 (12 ounce) package medium egg
  noodles, cooked, drained   340 g
1 (10 ounce) can cream of celery soup   280 g
1 (10 ounce) can cream of chicken soup   280 g
1 (15 ounce) can creamed corn   425 g
¾ cup half-and-half cream   180 ml
1½ cups corn flakes, crushed   360 ml
3 tablespoons butter, melted   45 ml

• Heat a little oil in skillet, brown and cook pork about
  15 minutes. Spoon pork into large bowl.

• With a little oil in skillet, saute celery, bell pepper and
  onion. Spoon into bowl with pork. Add noodles,
  both soups, creamed corn, half-and-half, and a little
  salt and pepper to pork.

• Mix well and pour into buttered 9 x 13-inch
  (23 x 33 cm) baking dish.

• Combine crushed corn flakes and butter and sprinkle
  over casserole. Bake covered at 350° (176° C) for
  about 30 minutes.

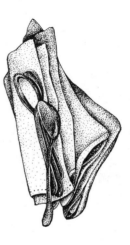

Oodles of Noodles

1½- 2 pounds pork tenderloin	1 kg
3 tablespoons oil	45 ml
2 cups celery, chopped	480 ml
1 green and 1 red bell pepper, seeded, chopped	
1 onion, chopped	
1 (4 ounce) can sliced mushrooms	114 g
1 (10 ounce) can tomatoes and green chilies	280 g
1 (10 ounce) can cream of mushroom soup with garlic	280 g
1 (10 ounce) can cream of celery soup	280 g
¼ cup soy sauce	60 ml
1 (7 ounce) package elbow macaroni, cooked, drained	198 g
2 cups chow mein noodles	480 ml

- Cut pork into 1-inch (2.5 cm) cubes. In skillet, brown pork in oil and cook on low heat for about 15 minutes. Remove pork with slotted spoon to side dish.

- Saute celery, bell peppers and onion in same skillet in remaining oil. In large bowl, combine pork, celery-onion mixture, mushrooms, tomatoes and green chilies, soups, soy sauce and macaroni.

- Spoon casserole into 1 large, buttered 9 x 13-inch (23 x 33 cm) baking dish or 2 smaller baking dishes. Top with chow mein noodles.

- Bake uncovered at 350° (176° C) for 50 minutes.

Tip: If you make 2 smaller casseroles, you may freeze one. Wait to sprinkle the chow mein noodles over casserole until just before you place it in the oven to cook.

Ham and Potatoes Olé!

1 (24 ounce) package frozen hash browns with onion and peppers, thawed	680 g
3 cups cubed, cooked ham	710 ml
1 (10 ounce) can cream of chicken soup	280 g
1 (10 ounce) can fiesta nacho cheese soup	280 g
1 cup hot salsa	240 ml
1 (8 ounce) package shredded cheddar-jack cheese	227 g

• Combine potatoes, ham, both soups and salsa in large bowl and mix well.

• Spoon into buttered 9 x 13-inch (23 x 33 cm) baking dish.

• Cover and cook at 350° (176° C) for 40 minutes.

• Remove from oven, sprinkle cheese over casserole and bake uncovered another 5 minutes.

Noodles-Ham Veggie Mix

1 (8 ounce) package medium egg noodles	227 g
1 (10 ounce) can cream of celery soup	280 g
1 (10 ounce) can cream of broccoli soup	280 g
1 teaspoon chicken bouillon	5 ml
1½ cups half-and-half cream	360 ml
1 (8 ounce) can whole kernel corn, drained	227 g
1 (16 ounce) package frozen broccoli, cauliflower and carrots, thawed	.5 kg
3 cups cooked cubed ham	710 ml
1 (8 ounce) package shredded cheddar-jack cheese, divided	227 g

• Cook noodles according to package directions and drain.

• In large bowl, combine soups, chicken bouillon, cream, corn, broccoli-carrot mixture, ham, ½ teaspoon (2 ml) each of salt and pepper and mix well.

• Fold in egg noodles and half of cheese.

• Spoon into greased 9 x 13-inch (23 x 33 cm) baking dish. Cover and bake at 350° (176° C) for 45 minutes.

• Uncover and sprinkle remaining cheese over top of casserole. Return to oven and bake another 10 minutes or until cheese bubbles.

Ham-It-Up Wild Rice

This is really simple to put together and the kids will be ready to eat their vegetables when they have ham and cheese with them.

1 (6 ounce) package instant long grain, wild rice	168 g
1 (10 ounce) package frozen broccoli spears, thawed	280 g
1 (8 ounce) can whole kernel corn, drained	227 g
3 cups, fully cooked, cubed ham	710 ml
1 (10 ounce) can cream of mushroom soup	280 g
1 cup mayonnaise	240 ml
1 teaspoon prepared mustard	5 ml
1 cup shredded cheddar cheese	240 ml
1 (3 ounce) can fried onion rings	84 g

• Prepare rice according to package directions.

• Spoon into buttered 3-quart (3 L) baking dish. Top with broccoli, corn and ham.

• In saucepan, combine soup, mayonnaise, mustard, shredded cheese and ½ teaspoon (2 ml) each of salt and pepper and mix well. Spread over top of rice-ham mixture.

• Cover and bake at 350° (176° C) for about 30 minutes. Remove from oven and sprinkle onion rings over top.

• Return to oven, uncovered, and bake additional 15 minutes or until casserole bubbles around edges and onion rings are light brown.

Tip: What a great way to use leftover ham, all the little slivers and chunks left from those nice big slices.

Walnut-Ham Linguine

2 teaspoons minced garlic	10 ml
½ cup coarsely chopped walnuts	120 ml
1 sweet red bell pepper, thinly sliced	
¼ cup olive oil	60 ml
½ pound cooked ham, cut in strips	227 g
1 (16 ounce) jar creamy alfredo sauce	.5 kg
¼ cup grated parmesan cheese	60 ml
1 (12 ounce) package linguine, cooked al dente	340 g
1 cup seasoned breadcrumbs	240 ml

• In large skillet, saute garlic, walnuts and bell pepper in oil for 1 to 2 minutes.

• In large bowl, combine garlic-bell pepper mixture, ham, alfredo sauce, parmesan cheese and linguine and mix well.

• Spoon into buttered 3-quart (3 L) baking dish. Sprinkle breadcrumbs over top.

• Bake uncovered at 350° (176° C) for 35 minutes or until breadcrumbs are light brown.

Sandwich Souffle

A fun lunch!

Butter, softened
8 slices white bread, crusts removed
4 slices ham
4 slices American cheese
2 cups milk   480 ml
2 eggs, beaten

- Butter bread on both sides, make 4 sandwiches with ham and cheese.

- Place sandwiches in buttered 8-inch (20 cm) square baking pan,

- Beat milk, eggs and a little salt and pepper. Pour over sandwiches and soak for 1 to 2 hours.

- Bake at 375° (190° C) for 45-50 minutes.

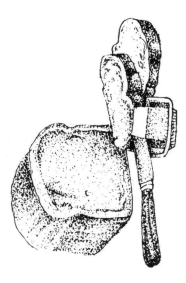

Ham-Cheese Bars

2 cups biscuit mix	480 ml
1 heaping cup cooked, finely chopped ham	240 ml
1 cup shredded cheddar cheese	240 ml
1/2 onion, finely chopped	
1/2 cup grated parmesan cheese	120 ml
1/4 cup sour cream	60 ml
1 teaspoon garlic powder	5 ml
1 cup whole milk	240 ml
1 egg	

- Combine all ingredients plus 1/2 teaspoon (2 ml) of salt in mixing bowl and mix by hand.

- Spread in a greased 9 x 13-inch (23 x 33 cm) baking pan. Bake at 350° (176° C) degrees for 30 minutes or until light brown.

- Cut in rectangles, about 2 x 1-inch (5 x 2.5 cm). Serve hot or room temperature.

Tip: This is not exactly a casserole, but it goes well with a lot of our brunch casseroles. They can be served at brunch or lunch and they can be kept in the refrigerator (cooked) and reheated. To reheat, place in a 325° (162° C) oven for about 15 minutes. They will be good and crispy when reheated.

Spectacular Ham-Asparagus Casserole

½ cup slivered almonds	120 ml
2 tablespoons butter, melted	30 ml
½ cup seasoned breadcrumbs	120 ml
1 pound fresh asparagus, trimmed	.5 kg
2 cups cooked, cubed ham	480 ml
½ cup grated cheddar cheese	120 ml
3 green onions, chopped	45 ml
½ cup fresh mushrooms, chopped	120 ml
3 tablespoons minced red bell pepper	45 ml
1 tablespoon lemon juice	15 ml
4 hard-boiled eggs, divided	
½ cup milk	120 ml
1 (10 ounce) cream of mushroom soup	280 g

- Toast almonds at 250° (121° C) for 15 minutes; set aside.

- Combine butter and breadcrumbs, toss; set aside.

- Arrange fresh asparagus in steamer basket and steam for 3 minutes.

- Drain, arrange asparagus in sprayed 1½-quart (1.5 L) baking dish and set aside.

- In mixing bowl combine ham, cheese, onion, mushrooms, almonds, bell pepper and lemon juice. Mix well.

- Carefully slice eggs into thin, diagonal pieces.

- Spoon layer of half ham mixture over asparagus and top with layer of half egg slices. Repeat layers.

- Combine milk and mushroom soup; blend well. Pour over ham mixture. Top with breadcrumbs.

- Bake at 350° (176° C) for 25 to 30 minutes.

Old-Fashioned Ham Loaf With Sassy Horseradish Sauce

3 eggs
3 pounds lean ground ham   1.3 kg
3 cups soft, fine breadcrumbs   710 ml
2 teaspoons brown sugar   10 ml
3 teaspoons prepared horseradish, divided   15 ml
½ pint whipping cream   227 g

- Slightly beat eggs in large mixing bowl.

- Stir in ground ham and mix thoroughly.

- Add breadcrumbs, brown sugar and 2 teaspoons (10 ml) horseradish and stir to mix well.

- Form into loaf and put in sprayed baking dish.

- Bake at 350° (176° C) for 1½ hours.

- Mix 1 teaspoon (5 ml) horseradish, ½ pint (227 g) whipping cream and a dash of salt and chill. Allow sauce to reach room temperature 20 minutes before serving.

- Remove loaf from oven, allow to set for about 5 minutes before slicing. Serve with sauce.

Seafood

Roughy Florentine

6 tablespoons butter, divided	90 ml
2 (10 ounce) boxes frozen spinach, thawed, drained	2 (280 g)
⅛ teaspoon ground nutmeg	.5 ml
2 pounds orange roughy fillets	1 kg
⅓ cup minced onion	80 ml
1 envelope cream of spinach soup mix	
1 pint half-and half-cream	.5 kg
2 cups shredded Swiss cheese	480 ml

- Heat 3 tablespoons (45 ml) butter in large skillet and cook spinach for about 2 minutes. Season with nutmeg and ½ teaspoon (2 ml) each of salt and pepper.

- Spoon spinach into buttered 9 x 13-inch (23 x 33 cm) baking dish and spread spinach over bottom of dish.

- Lay orange roughy over the spinach.

- In saucepan heat 3 tablespoons (45 ml) butter and saute onion. Add soup mix, cream and cheese and mix well. Heat just until cheese melts.

- Pour sauce over fillets and spinach.

- Cover and bake at 350° (176° C) for 20 to 25 minutes or until fillets flake easily and sauce is bubbly.

Crab-Stuffed Orange Roughy

⅓ cup seasoned breadcrumbs	80 ml
1 egg, beaten	
1 tablespoon finely minced onion	15 ml
2 tablespoons finely minced sweet	
red bell pepper	30 ml
1 teaspoon Creole seasoning	5 ml
1 teaspoon dry mustard	5 ml
1 teaspoon dried parsley flakes	5 ml
Scant teaspoon hot sauce	
2 (6 ounce) cans crabmeat, drained, flaked	2 (168 g)
8 (5 ounce) orange roughy fillets	8 (143 g)
3 tablespoons butter	45 ml
2 tablespoons lemon juice	30 ml
¼ teaspoon lemon juice	1 ml
Commercial mornay sauce	
Hot cooked rice	

- Combine breadcrumbs, egg, onion, bell pepper, seasoning, mustard, parsley flakes and a little hot sauce in bowl and mix well. Add crabmeat and stir gently.
- Spoon ¼ cup (60 ml) crabmeat mixture onto each fillet. Roll fillet to enclose filling. Place fillet rolls, seam-side down, in buttered 9 x 13-inch (23 x 33 cm) baking dish. Place a little dot of butter on each fillet and sprinkle with lemon juice and a little paprika, if you have it.
- Bake uncovered at 350° (176° C) for 30 minutes or until fish flakes easily when tested with fork.
- Place rolls on bed of rice and serve with mornay sauce.

Tip: In case you cannot find the commercial mornay sauce use our recipe on page 232.

Mornay Sauce:

1 tablespoon butter	15 ml
1 tablespoon flour	15 ml
1 cup milk	240 ml
1 egg yolk, beaten	
2 tablespoons whipping cream	30 ml
3 tablespoons shredded Swiss cheese	45 ml
2 tablespoons grated parmesan cheese	30 ml

• Melt butter, add flour and cook about 1 minute, stirring constantly. Gradually add milk, ½ teaspoon (2 ml) salt and cook, stirring constantly until mixture thickens.

• Combine egg yolk and whipping cream and very gradually add a little at a time to hot mixture, stirring constantly, until thick.

• Remove from heat, add cheeses and stir until cheese melts.

Creamy Orange Roughy

½ cup (1 stick) butter, divided	120 ml
1 sweet red bell pepper, chopped	
1 onion, chopped	
¼ cup flour	60 ml
1 teaspoon basil	5 ml
1 pint half-and-half cream	.5 kg
1 (3 ounce) package grated parmesan cheese	84 g
1 tablespoon white wine	
Worcestershire sauce	15 ml
1½ pounds orange roughy fillets	680 g
3 hard-boiled eggs, sliced	
1½ cups round buttery cracker crumbs	360 ml

- Melt 4 tablespoons (60 ml) butter in skillet and saute bell pepper and onion.

- Add flour, basil, ½ teaspoon (2 ml) each of salt and pepper to skillet and cook on medium heat about 2 minutes. Slowly add cream, stirring constantly, until mixture thickens.

- Stir in parmesan cheese and white wine Worcestershire.

- Melt 2 tablespoons (30 ml) butter in another skillet and brown orange roughy fillet. Transfer to greased 9 x 13-inch (23 x 33 cm) baking dish and place egg slices over fish.

- Pour cream sauce over eggs and fillets.

- Bake uncovered at 350° (176° C) for 15 minutes.

- Combine cracker crumbs and remaining 2 tablespoons (30 ml) butter.

- Sprinkle crumbs over casserole and bake another 10 to 15 minutes or until crumbs are light brown.

Tip: *You may substitute any white fish for the orange roughy.*

Crabmeat Special

½ cup celery, chopped	120 ml
1 cup onion, chopped	240 ml
½ cup red bell pepper, chopped	120 ml
¼ cup (½ stick) butter	60 ml
2 tablespoons flour	30 ml
1 pint half-and-half cream	.5 kg
1 egg, beaten	
2½ teaspoons Cajun seasoning	12 ml
1 cup cooked white rice	240 ml
1 pound fresh crabmeat, flaked, shredded	.5 kg
1 cup shredded cheddar cheese	240 ml

- Saute celery, onion and red bell pepper in skillet with butter, but do not brown. Blend in flour over low heat.

- Gradually add cream, egg, Cajun seasoning and 1½ teaspoons (7 ml) salt and ¼ teaspoon (1 ml) cayenne or pepper. Cook on medium heat, stirring constantly, about 5 minutes, until mixture thickens.

- Fold in rice and crabmeat and blend well. Spoon into buttered 2-quart (2 L) baking dish.

- Bake covered at 325° (162° C) for 20 minutes or until bubbly. Uncover and sprinkle cheese over top of casserole.

- Return to oven for about 5 minutes, just until cheese melts.

Tip: The fresh crabmeat may be substituted for 2 (8 ounce/227 g) cartons Louis Kemp crab delights in refrigerated section of your grocery store.

No-Panic Crab Casserole

2 (6 ounce) cans crabmeat, drained, flaked	2 (168 g)
1 cup half-and-half cream	240 ml
1½ cups mayonnaise	360 ml
6 hard-boiled eggs, finely chopped	
1 cup seasoned breadcrumbs, divided	240 ml
1 tablespoon dried parsley flakes	15 ml
½ teaspoon dried basil	2 ml
1 (8 ounce) can sliced water chestnuts, drained	227 g
2 tablespoons butter, melted	30 ml

- Combine crabmeat, cream, mayonnaise, hard-boiled eggs, ½ cup (120 ml) seasoned breadcrumbs, parsley, basil, water chestnuts and a little salt and pepper in bowl and mix well. Pour into buttered 2-quart (2 L) baking dish.

- Combine remaining ½ cup (120 ml) breadcrumbs and butter and sprinkle over top of casserole.

- Bake uncovered at 350° (176° C) for 40 minutes.

Crab-Stuffed Baked Potatoes

If you have been looking for a baked potato that is truly a meal in itself, this is it!

4 large baking potatoes	
½ cup (1 stick) butter	120 ml
½ cup whipping cream	120 ml
1 bunch fresh green onions, chopped	
2 (6 ounce) cans crabmeat, drained, flaked	2 (168 g)
¾ cup shredded cheddar cheese	180 ml
2 tablespoons fresh minced parsley	30 ml

• Bake potatoes at 375° (190° C) for 1 hour or until well done. Half each potato lengthwise and scoop out pulp but leave skins intact.

• In large bowl, mash potatoes with butter. Add whipping cream, green onions and ¾ teaspoon (4 ml) salt and ½ teaspoon (2 ml) pepper. Stir in crabmeat.

• Fill reserved potato skins with potato mixture. Sprinkle with cheese.

• Bake at 350° (176° C) for about 15 minutes.

• To serve, sprinkle fresh parsley over cheese.

Fettuccine of the Sea

¼ cup (½ stick) butter	60 ml
¼ cup flour	60 ml
1 teaspoon Creole seasoning	5 ml
1 tablespoon minced garlic	15 ml
1 (16 ounce) carton half-and-half cream	.5 kg
½ cup milk	120 ml
½ cup red bell pepper, finely chopped	120 ml
2 (6 ounce) cans tiny shrimp, picked, veined	2 (168 g)
2 (6 ounce) cans crabmeat, drained, flaked	2 (168 g)
1 (6 ounce) can chopped clams, drained	168 g
½ cup grated parmesan cheese	120 ml
1 (12 ounce) package fettuccine, cooked al dente	340 g

• Melt butter in saucepan and add flour, Creole seasoning, 3/4 teaspoon (4 ml) pepper and garlic and mix well. On medium heat, gradually add cream and milk and mix well. Cook, stirring constantly, until it thickens.

• Add bell pepper, shrimp, crabmeat, clams and parmesan cheese and heat thoroughly.

• In buttered 9 x 13-inch (23 x 33 cm) baking dish, spoon half fettuccine in bottom of dish and half seafood sauce. Repeat layers.

• Cover and bake at 325° (162° C) for 25 minutes or just until casserole bubbles.

Seafood Lasagna

8 lasagna noodles, cooked	
2 tablespoons butter	30 ml
1 onion, chopped	
1 (8 ounce) package cream cheese, softened	227 g
1 (15 ounce) carton ricotta cheese	425 g
1 (4 ounce) jar chopped pimentos, drained	114 g
1 egg, beaten	
2 teaspoons dried basil	10 ml
1 (10 ounce) can cream of shrimp soup	280 g
1 (10 ounce) can fiesta nacho cheese soup	280 g
½ cup milk	120 ml
1 pound small, cooked shrimp, peeled, veined	.5 kg
2 (6 ounce) cans crabmeat, drained, flaked	2 (168 g)
1 cup shredded cheddar cheese	240 ml

- In large skillet melt butter and saute onion until tender. Stir in cream cheese, ricotta cheese, pimentos, egg, basil and salt to taste.

- In saucepan, combine both soups and milk; heat just to mix well. Add shrimp and crabmeat.

- In greased 9 x 13-inch (23 x 33 cm) baking dish, layer four noodles.

- Spread half of the cream cheese-pimento mixture over noodles and top with half seafood mixture. Repeat layers with remaining four noodles, cream cheese-pimento mixture, then seafood mixture.

- Cover and bake at 350° (176° C) for 45 minutes.

- Remove from oven, top with cheddar cheese and return to oven for 3 to 4 minutes.

Seafood Imperial

10 slices white bread, crust removed,
  cubed, divided
1 (16 ounce) package imitation crabmeat,
  cubed, divided .5 kg
2 (6 ounce) cans tiny shrimp, drained,
  veined 2 (168 g)
1 cup mayonnaise 240 ml
1 cup celery, chopped 240 ml
1 sweet red bell pepper, chopped
1 teaspoon dried parsley flakes 5 ml
1 teaspoon lemon juice 5 ml
5 eggs, beaten
3½ cups milk, divided 830 ml
1 (10 ounce) can golden mushroom soup 280 g
¾ cup grated parmesan cheese 180 ml

- Place half bread cubes in bottom of greased
  11 x 14-inch (30 x 36 cm) baking dish.

- Combine crabmeat, shrimp, mayonnaise, celery, bell
  pepper, parsley flakes, lemon juice and ½ teaspoon
  (2 ml) pepper in bowl.

- Spread seafood mixture over bread cubes. Sprinkle
  remaining bread cubes over seafood mixture.

- In large bowl, combine eggs and 3 cups (710 ml) milk
  and beat well. Slowly pour eggs and milk over bread
  cubes.

- Cover and refrigerate 4 to 5 hours or overnight.

- Bake covered at 325° (162° C) for 1 hour.

- Combine mushroom soup, ½ cup milk (120 ml) and
  parmesan cheese in saucepan and heat just to mix well.

- Remove casserole from oven and pour soup mixture
  over casserole.

- Bake uncovered at 400° (204° C) for 10 minutes.

Neptune Lasagna

3 tablespoons butter	45 ml
1 sweet red bell pepper, chopped	
1 onion, chopped	
1 (8 ounce) package cream cheese, softened	227 g
1 (12 ounce) carton small curd cottage cheese	340 g
1 egg, beaten	
2 teaspoons dried basil	10 ml
2 teaspoons Creole seasoning	10 ml
1 (10 ounce) can cream of shrimp soup	280 g
1 (10 ounce) can cream of celery soup	280 g
2 teaspoons dried basil	10 ml
½ cup white wine	120 ml
¾ cup milk	180 ml
2 (8 ounce) packages imitation crabmeat	2 (227 g)
2 (6 ounce) packages small shrimp, rinsed, drained	2 (168 g)
9 lasagna noodles, cooked, drained	
1 (3 ounce) package grated parmesan cheese	84 g
1 cup shredded white cheddar cheese	240 ml

- Heat butter in skillet and saute bell pepper and onion. Reduce heat. Add cream cheese and stir until cream cheese melts. Remove from heat and add cottage cheese, egg, basil, ½ teaspoon (2 ml) pepper and Creole seasoning and set aside.

- In bowl combine both soups, basil, white wine, milk, crabmeat and shrimp and mix well.

- Butter 9 x 13-inch (23 x 33 cm) baking dish and arrange 3 noodles. Spread with one-third of cottage cheese mixture and one-third seafood mixture. Repeat layers twice. Sprinkle with parmesan cheese.

- Cover and bake at 350° (176° C) for about 40 minutes.

- Uncover and sprinkle with white cheddar cheese and bake 10 minutes longer or until casserole bubbles. Let stand for at least 15 minutes before serving.

Seafood Royale

1 cup uncooked rice	240 ml
2 (10 ounce) cans cream of shrimp soup	2 (280 g)
1 cup milk	240 ml
⅔ cup mayonnaise	160 ml
1 teaspoon Creole seasoning	5 ml
3 pounds cooked, peeled shrimp	1.3 kg
1 (6 ounce) can crabmeat, drained, flaked	168 g
1 onion, chopped	
2 cups celery, chopped	480 ml
4 tablespoons snipped parsley	60 ml
1 (8 ounce) can sliced water chestnuts, drained	227 g
½ cup slivered almonds	120 ml

- Cook rice according to package directions until fluffy.

- In large bowl, combine soup, milk and mayonnaise and mix well.

- Add shrimp, crabmeat, onion, celery, parsley, water chestnuts and ½ teaspoon (2 ml) each of salt and pepper.

- Fold in rice and mix well.

- Pour into buttered 3-quart (3 L) baking dish and sprinkle almonds over top of casserole.

- Bake covered at 325° (162° C) for 25 minutes, uncover and bake additional 10 minutes.

Lasagna
Down-Mexico-Way

1 pound uncooked medium shrimp, peeled, veined	.5 kg
2 teaspoons minced garlic	10 ml
1 sweet red bell pepper, chopped	
2 tablespoons olive oil	30 ml
5 tablespoons butter	75 ml
⅓ cup flour	80 ml
1 teaspoon seafood seasoning	5 ml
1 cup chicken broth	240 ml
1 (8 ounce) carton whipping cream	227 g
1 (16 ounce) jar hot chunky salsa	.5 kg
12 (6-inch) corn tortillas, cut in strips	12 (15 cm)
1 (16 ounce) package imitation crabmeat	.5 kg
1 (12 ounce) package Monterey Jack cheese	340 g

- Cook shrimp, garlic and bell pepper in oil in skillet until shrimp turns pink. Remove from skillet.

- In same skillet, melt butter and stir in flour and seasoning until smooth.

- On medium high heat, gradually add broth and stir until sauce thickens. Stir in cream and salsa and heat thoroughly.

- Spread ½ cup (120 ml) sauce in buttered 9 x 13-inch (23 x 33 cm) baking pan.

- Layer with half tortilla strips, half shrimp-bell pepper mixture, half crab, half sauce and half cheese. Repeat layers, leaving off last half of cheese.

- Bake covered at 350° (176° C) for 35 minutes. Uncover and sprinkle remaining cheese over top of casserole. Return to oven for 5 minutes before serving.

Shrimp and Artichokes

1 onion, chopped	
1 cup celery, diagonally chopped	240 ml
1 teaspoon minced garlic	5 ml
2 sweet red bell peppers, thinly sliced	
1 green bell pepper, thinly sliced	
½ cup (1 stick) butter	120 ml
3 pounds shrimp, boiled, peeled, veined	1.3 kg
3½ cups cooked white rice	830 ml
½ cup tomato sauce	120 ml
1 (8 ounce) carton whipping cream	227 g
¼ teaspoon cayenne pepper	1 ml
1 teaspoon Creole seasoning	5 ml
2 (14 ounce) cans artichoke hearts, drained, halved	2 (396 g)
1 (8 ounce) package shredded cheddar cheese	227 g

- Saute onion, celery, garlic, bell peppers in large skillet in butter, but be careful not to brown.

- Add cooked shrimp, rice, tomato sauce, cream, cayenne pepper and Creole seasoning and mix well. Fold in artichoke hearts.

- Spoon into buttered 11 x 14-inch (30 x 36 cm) baking dish. Cover and bake at 350° (176° C) for 20 minutes.

- Uncover and sprinkle cheese over top of casserole and return to oven for about 10 minutes.

Savory Shrimp Fettuccine

2 tablespoons butter	30 ml
⅓ cup onion, chopped	80 ml
1 teaspoon seafood seasoning	5 ml
½ pound small shrimp, peeled, veined	227 g
1 (10 ounce) can cream of shrimp soup	280 g
½ cup half-and-half cream	120 ml
½ cup mayonnaise	120 ml
2 teaspoons white wine Worcestershire sauce	10 ml
½ teaspoon prepared horseradish	2 ml
1 cup grated white cheddar cheese, divided	240 ml
2 cups cooked fettuccine	480 ml
1 (16 ounce) package frozen broccoli florets, cooked	.5 kg

• In large saucepan, melt butter and saute onion. Add seasoning and shrimp and cook, while stirring until shrimp turns pink, about 2 minutes.

• Add shrimp soup, cream, mayonnaise, Worcestershire, horseradish and half cheese. Heat just until cheese melts.

• Fold in fettuccine.

• When broccoli cools from cooking, cut some stems away and discard. Fold broccoli into sauce. Spoon into buttered 3-quart (3 L) baking dish. Cover and bake at 350° (176° C) for 30 minutes.

• Remove from oven and sprinkle remaining cheese on top. Bake 5 minutes longer.

The Captain's Shrimp and Eggs

¼ cup (½ stick) butter	60 ml
1 bunch fresh green onions, with tops, sliced	
5 tablespoons flour	75 ml
½ cup dry white wine	120 ml
1 (8 ounce) carton whipping cream	227 g
¾ cup milk	180 ml
2 teaspoons dried dill weed	10 ml
⅔ cup shredded cheddar cheese	160 ml
16 hard-boiled eggs	
1½ pounds shrimp, boiled, peeled, veined	680 g
1½ cups fresh breadcrumbs	360 ml
5 tablespoons butter, melted	75 ml
¾ cup grated parmesan cheese	180 ml

• Saute green onions in medium skillet in butter. Stir in flour and cook 1 minute, stirring constantly, but do not brown.

• Add wine, cream, milk and dill weed, cook on medium heat, and stir constantly until sauce thickens.

• Stir in cheddar cheese and set aside.

• Cut eggs in half lengthwise. Place eggs, yolk side up, in 9 x 13-inch (23 x 33 cm) baking dish. Cover with shrimp.

• Slowly pour sauce on top of shrimp.

• Mix breadcrumbs, butter and parmesan cheese in bowl. Sprinkle on top of casserole.

• Bake uncovered at 375° (190° C) for 20 minutes or until hot and bubbly.

No Ordinary Shrimp

½ cup sweet onion, chopped	120 ml
1 red bell pepper, thinly sliced	
5 tablespoons butter, divided	75 ml
2 tablespoons flour	30 ml
¾ cup half-and-half cream	180 ml
1 teaspoon white wine Worcestershire	5 ml
3 cups cooked, peeled, veined shrimp	710 ml
2 cups cooked white rice	480 ml
¾ cup shredded cheddar cheese	180 ml
¾ cup butter cracker crumbs	180 ml

- Saute onion and bell pepper in 3 tablespoons (45 ml) butter in skillet, but do not brown.

- Blend in flour, ½ teaspoon (2 ml) each of salt and pepper, heat, and mix well.

- On medium heat, gradually stir in cream and Worcestershire and stir until it thickens. Fold in mushrooms and shrimp.

- Place cooked rice in buttered 7 x 11-inch (18 x 28 cm) baking dish and spread out. Pour shrimp mixture over rice.

- Sprinkle cheese over top and combine cracker crumbs and melted butter. Sprinkle over casserole.

- Bake uncovered at 350° (176° C) for about 20 to 25 minutes or until crumbs are light brown.

Shrimp Delight

1½ pounds raw shrimp	680 g
Shrimp boil	
2 tablespoons (¼ stick) butter	30 ml
1 onion, chopped	
1 red and 1 green bell pepper, chopped	
1 teaspoon minced garlic	5 ml
1 (10 ounce) can cream of shrimp soup	280 g
1 (10 ounce) can cream of celery soup	280 g
2 cups cooked rice	480 ml
1 teaspoon Creole seasoning	5 ml
1 cup potato chips, crushed	240 ml

• Cook shrimp in shrimp boil according to package directions. Cool, peel and vein. Saute onion, bell peppers and garlic in large skillet with butter.

• In large bowl, combine shrimp, onion-pepper mixture, soups, rice, ¾ teaspoon (4 ml) pepper and Creole seasoning and mix well.

• Spoon into greased casserole dish and sprinkle with potato chips. Bake at 350° (176° C) for 30 minutes.

Salmon Casserole

6 ounces dried egg noodles	168 g
1 (10 ounce) can cream of celery soup	280 g
1 (5 ounce) can evaporated milk	143 g
1 tablespoon lemon juice	15 ml
½ onion, chopped	
1 (15 ounce) can salmon, skin, boneless	425 g
1 cup shredded cheddar cheese	240 ml
1 (8 ounce) can small green peas, drained	227 g
1 teaspoon Creole seasoning	5 ml
1 cup cheese crackers, crushed	240 ml
2 tablespoons butter, melted	30 ml

- Cook noodles according to package directions and drain.

- Stir in soup, milk, lemon juice, onion, salmon, cheese, peas, Creole seasoning and 1 teaspoon (5 ml) salt.

- Spoon into greased 7 x 11-inch (18 x 28 cm) baking dish.

- Bake covered at 350° (176° C) for 25 minutes.

- Combine cheese crackers and melted butter and sprinkle over casserole and return to oven for 10 minutes or until crumbs are lightly brown.

Tuna-In-the-Straw

1 (8 ounce) package egg noodles	227 g
2 (10 ounce) cans cream of chicken soup	2 (280 g)
1 (8 ounce) carton sour cream	227 g
1 teaspoon Creole seasoning	5 ml
½ cup milk	120 ml
2 (6 ounce) cans white meat tuna, drained	2 (168 g)
1 cup shredded processed cheese	240 ml
1 (10 ounce) box green peas, thawed	280 g
1 (2 ounce) jar diced pimento	57 g
1 (2 ounce) can shoe-string potatoes	57 g

• Cook noodles according to package directions and drain.

• In large bowl, combine soup, sour cream, Creole seasoning and milk and mix well.

• Add noodles, tuna, cheese, peas and pimento.

• Pour into greased 9 x 13-inch (23 x 33 cm) baking dish. Sprinkle top with shoe-string potatoes.

• Bake uncovered at 350° (176° C) for about 35 minutes or until shoe-string potatoes are light brown.

No-Noodle Tuna

1 (8 ounce) tube refrigerated crescent rolls	227 g
1 cup shredded white cheddar cheese	240 ml
1 (10 ounce) box frozen chopped broccoli, thawed	280 g
4 eggs, beaten	
1 (2 ounce) box cream of broccoli soup mix	57 g
1 (8 ounce) carton sour cream	227 g
1 cup milk	240 ml
½ cup mayonnaise	120 ml
2 tablespoons dried onion flakes	30 ml
½ teaspoon dill weed	2 ml
2 (6 ounce) cans white meat tuna, drained	2 (168 g)
1 (2 ounce) jar diced pimentos	57 g

- Unroll crescent dough into 1 long rectangle and place in ungreased 9 x 13-inch (23 x 33 cm) baking dish. Seal seams and press onto bottom and ½-inch (1.2 cm) up sides.

- Sprinkle with cheese and chopped broccoli.

- In bowl, combine eggs, broccoli soup mix, sour cream, milk, mayonnaise, onion flakes and dill weed and mix well.

- Stir in tuna and pimentos. Pour over broccoli-cheese in baking dish.

- Bake covered at 350° (176° C) for 40 minutes or until knife inserted near center comes out clean. Cut in squares to serve.

Georgia-Oyster Casserole

2 pints oysters	1 kg
½ cup (1 stick) butter, divided	120 ml
3 whole scallions, chopped	
1 cup green bell peppers, chopped	240 ml
1½ cups fresh sliced mushrooms	360 ml
¼ cup flour	60 ml
1 (8 ounce) carton whipping cream	227 g
1 (3 ounce) package grated parmesan cheese	84 g
¾ cup seasoned breadcrumbs	180 ml

- Drain oysters and set aside. Saute scallions and pepper in large skillet with 2 tablespoons (30 ml) butter until tender.

- Add mushrooms and oysters and saute for 5 minutes.

- Melt 2 tablespoons (30 ml) butter over medium low heat in saucepan. Add flour and stir well. Slowly add cream, stirring constantly, until sauce thickens.

- Fold in cheese, mix well and pour cheese sauce into oyster mixture. Season with ½ teaspoon (2 ml) each of salt and pepper. Simmer for 3 to 5 minutes.

- Spoon mixture into buttered 9 x 13-inch (23 x 33 cm) baking dish. Sprinkle breadcrumbs over top and dot with remaining butter. Place under broiler and brown until casserole bubbles. Watch closely.

Fettuccine A La Crawfish

1 (12 ounce) package fettuccine   340 g

3 bell peppers, chopped
3 onions, chopped
6 ribs celery, chopped
1½ cups (3 sticks) butter   360 ml
1 (14 ounce) package frozen crawfish tails   396 g
    thawed, drained
2 tablespoons snipped parsley   30 ml
4-5 cloves garlic, minced
1 pint half-and-half cream   .5 kg
½ cup flour   120 ml
1 (1 pound) package jalapeno cheese, cubed   .5 kg

- Cook noodles according to package directions. Drain and set aside.

- Saute bell pepper, onion and celery in butter.

- Add crawfish tails, simmer for 8 to 10 minutes and stir occasionally.

- Add parsley, garlic and half-and-half and mix well. Gradually stir in flour and mix well. Simmer for 30 minutes and stir occasionally.

- Add cheese and continue to stir until it melts and blends. Mix fettuccine with sauce.

- Pour all into sprayed 6-quart (6 L) baking dish. Bake at 300° (148° C) for 15 to 20 minutes or until it is hot.

Salads

Crunchy Chinese Slaw

This recipe is so good and it will go with just about any main dish. And it will serve a bunch of people probably 18 to 20. The beauty of this recipe is that you will hope you have some leftovers!

1 cup slivered almonds		240 ml
2 (16 ounce) packages shredded slaw mix		2 (.5 kg)
1 bunch green onions, sliced		
1 green and 1 red bell pepper, finely diced		
1 cup celery, sliced		240 ml
1 (11 ounce) can mandarin oranges, drained		312 g
2 packages chicken-flavored ramen noodles, crumbled		
1 cup sunflower seeds		240 ml

Dressing:

1 cup oil	240 ml
3/4 cup white vinegar	180 ml
3/4 cup sugar	180 ml
2 dashes hot sauce	
Ramen noodles' seasoning packet	

- Toast slivered almonds at 275° (135° C) for about 12 minutes.

- In large bowl, combine slaw mix, toasted almonds, onions, bell peppers, celery, oranges, ramen noodles and sunflower seeds and mix well.

- In pint jar, combine oil, vinegar, sugar, hot sauce, seasoning packet and 2 teaspoons (10 ml) salt and 1 teaspoon (5 ml) pepper and mix well.

- Spoon over slaw ingredients and toss well. Refrigerate.

Tip: This slaw can certainly be made ahead of time and it will keep in the refrigerator for several days.

Cauliflower-Broccoli Salad

This is another salad that makes a bunch, probably serving 18 to 20. It may be made a day ahead, but you would not want to keep it more than 2 or 3 days in the refrigerator. It is really a great salad for a lot of people and you have 5 different vegetables all in one bowl.

1 (8 ounce) carton sour cream	227 g
1 cup mayonnaise	240 ml
1 package original Ranch dressing mix	
1 head cauliflower, cut into bite-size pieces	
1 bunch fresh broccoli, broken into bite-size pieces	
1 (10 ounce) box frozen green peas, thawed	280 g
3 ribs celery, sliced	
1 bunch green onions, with tops, chopped	
1 (8 ounce) can sliced water chestnuts, drained	227 g
⅓ cup sweet relish, drained	80 ml
8-10 ounces mozzarella cheese, cubed	280 g
½ cup slivered almonds, toasted	120 ml

• Mix sour cream, mayonnaise and dressing mix and set aside.

• Wash cauliflower and broccoli and drain well on paper towels. (They should be dry).

• Combine cauliflower, broccoli, green peas, celery, onions, water chestnuts and sweet relish in large bowl and mix well. Add dressing and toss. Refrigerate.

Artichoke Salad

1 envelope plain gelatin	
1 cup mayonnaise*	240 ml
1 (14 ounce) can hearts of artichoke, well drained	396 g
½ (10 ounce) package frozen green peas, thawed	½ (280 g)
2 tablespoons lemon juice	30 ml
1 (4 ounce) jar chopped pimentos	114 g
1 bunch green onion, with tops, finely chopped	
1½ cups shredded mozzarella cheese	360 ml
1 teaspoon Italian herb seasoning	5 ml
½ teaspoon garlic powder	2 ml

- Soften gelatin in (¼ cup/60 ml) cold water. Add (½ cup/120 ml) boiling water and mix well.

- Add mayonnaise and stir until smooth.

- Remove any spikes or tough leaves from artichoke hearts, chop and stir into gelatin.

- Add all remaining ingredients with ½ teaspoon (2 ml) salt. Pour into ring mold and refrigerate.

- When ready to serve, slip a knife around edges to loosen from mold. Unmold onto a serving plate lined with lettuce.

Tip: Do not use salad dressing. Mayonnaise really makes a difference.

Tip: For a pretty finish, sprinkle a little paprika over salad. You can place olives, black olives or radishes in center of ring.

Winter Salad

When you need a quick "something" to take to a friend, this is it! And it can be kept in the refrigerator for a week. It's a really good salad to have on hand.

1 (15 ounce) can cut green beans, drained	425 g
1 (15 ounce) can jalapeno black-eyed peas, drained	425 g
1 (15 ounce) can shoe-peg white corn, drained	425 g
1 (15 ounce) can green peas, drained	425 g
1 (4 ounce) jar chopped pimentos	114 g
1 sweet red bell pepper, chopped	

- Combine all vegetables in 3-quart (3 L) container with lid and mix well.

Dressing:

¾ cup sugar	180 ml
½ cup oil	120 ml
¾ cup white vinegar	180 ml
¾ teaspoon garlic powder	4 ml

- Add all dressing ingredients with 2 teaspoons (10 ml) salt and 1 teaspoon (5 ml) pepper in small bowl and mix well. Pour over vegetables, mix well, cover and refrigerate.

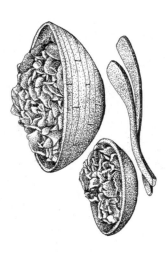

Crunchy Pea Salad

1 (16 ounce) package frozen green peas, thawed .5 kg

½ head cauliflower, cut into small florets

1 cup celery, chopped 240 ml

1 (8 ounce) can water chestnuts, drained 227 g

1 (4 ounce) jar pimentos, drained 114 g

1½ cups mayonnaise 360 ml

¼ cup Italian dressing 60 ml

1 cup peanuts 240 ml

½ cup bacon bits 120 ml

- Combine peas, cauliflower, celery, water chestnuts, pimentos and about 1 teaspoon (5 ml) salt in large bowl.

- Mix mayonnaise and Italian dressing. Combine with salad, cover and refrigerate.

- When ready to serve, add peanuts and toss, well.

- Place in pretty crystal bowl and sprinkle bacon bits over top as garnish.

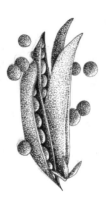

Black-Eyed Pea Salad

2 (15 ounce) cans jalapeno black-eyed peas,
  drained   2 (425 g)
1 ripe avocado, peeled, chopped
1 purple onion, chopped
1 cup celery, chopped   240 ml
1 red and 1 green bell pepper, chopped

Dressing:
⅓ cup oil   80 ml
⅓ cup white vinegar   80 ml
3 tablespoons sugar   45 ml
¼ teaspoon garlic powder   1 ml

- In large bowl, mix all salad ingredients. (It would be a good idea if you sprinkled a little lemon juice over the avocado as you peel it.)

- Combine dressing ingredients with ½ teaspoon (2 ml) salt and mix well.

- Add dressing to vegetables and toss. Cover and refrigerate. Onion, celery and peppers will stay crisp in the refrigerator several days, so omit avocado if you don't plan to serve the same day.

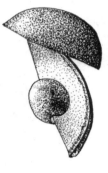

Calico Salad

1 (15 ounce) can whole kernel white corn, drained	425 g
1 (15 ounce) can green peas, drained	425 g
1 (8 ounce) can whole green beans, drained	227 g
1 (15 ounce) can garbanzo beans, drained	425 g
1 cup celery, chopped	240 ml
1 sweet red bell pepper, chopped	
1 bunch fresh green onion, with tops, sliced	
1 (2 ounce) jar chopped pimento, drained	57 g

Dressing:

½ cup sugar	120 ml
½ cup wine vinegar	120 ml
½ cup oil	120 ml
½ teaspoon basil	2 ml
1 tablespoon white wine Worcestershire sauce	15 ml

- Drain all vegetables and combine in bowl with lid.

- Mix dressing ingredients with 1 teaspoon (5 ml) salt and ½ teaspoon (2 ml) pepper thoroughly and pour over vegetables.

- Cover and refrigerate overnight. This will keep several days in refrigerator.

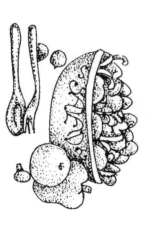

Layered Company Salad

1 (10 ounce) package fresh spinach, torn into pieces	280 g
1 cup sliced fresh mushrooms	240 ml
1 bunch green onions, with tops, chopped	
1 (10 ounce) box frozen green peas, thawed	280 g
3 ribs celery, sliced	
1½ cups shredded cheddar cheese	360 ml
2 teaspoons sugar, divided	10 ml
4 hard-boiled eggs, grated	
1 sweet red bell pepper, chopped	
1 cucumber, sliced	
½ head cauliflower, chopped	
1 cup shredded Monterey Jack cheese	240 ml

Dressing:

1½ cups mayonnaise	360 ml
1½ cups sour cream	360 ml

• For this salad, use only half the spinach for first layer in the bottom of a large bowl, then place a layer mushrooms, green onions, peas, celery and half cheddar cheese.

• In bowl combine mayonnaise and sour cream for dressing and spread half over top of cheese. Sprinkle with 1 teaspoon (5 ml) sugar, a little salt and lots of pepper.

• Next layer remaining spinach, eggs, bell pepper, cucumber, cauliflower and remaining cheddar cheese. Spread remaining dressing on top. Sprinkle 1 teaspoon (5 ml) sugar, a little salt and pepper. Top with Monterey Jack cheese.

• Cover with plastic wrap and refrigerate overnight.

A large crystal bowl about 10 inches (25 cm) in diameter will make this a spectacular dish.

Wonderful Broccoli Salad

When I first saw this salad, I thought, "Raisins in my salad — no way!" but I was wrong. Now this is my favorite salad.

1 large bunch fresh broccoli	
½ purple onion, sliced, separated	
½ cup golden raisins	120 ml
½ cup slivered almonds, toasted	120 ml
½ cup celery, chopped	120 ml

Dressing:

1 cup mayonnaise	240 ml
¼ cup sugar	60 ml
2 tablespoons vinegar	30 ml

- Wash your broccoli ahead of time and drain well on paper towels. (The broccoli needs to be well-drained.) Cut into small bite-size florets.

- In large bowl, combine broccoli, onion, raisins, almonds and celery and mix well. (The sliced and separated onion looks better, but chopped onion is easier to eat.)

- Combine the dressing ingredients with 1 teaspoon (5 ml) salt and ½ teaspoon (2 ml) pepper. Spoon over broccoli mixture and toss. Refrigerate several hours before serving.

- Sprinkle bacon bits over salad just before serving

Tip: *You can make this salad a day ahead. Remarkably the broccoli stays crisp for several days (however I wouldn't keep it longer than 2 or 3 days because of the mayonnaise).*

Notes

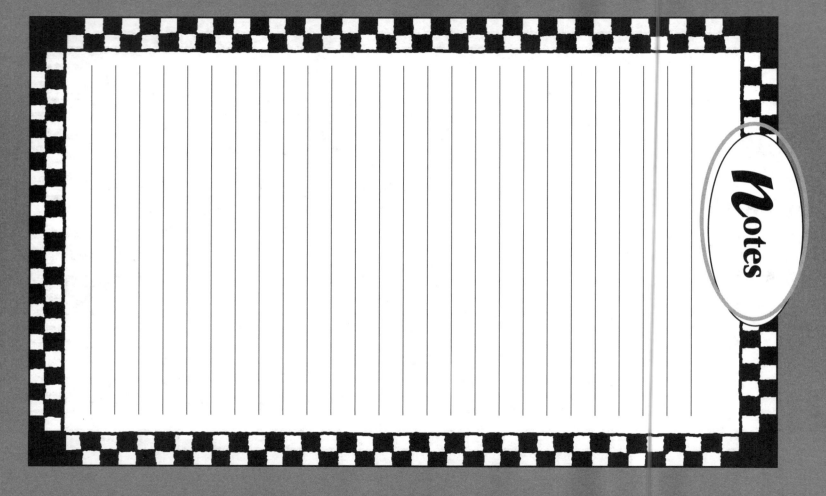

Notes

Grocery List

Fresh Bakery

— Bagels
— Bread
— Cake
— Cookies
— Croissants
— Donuts
— French Bread
— Muffins
— Pastries
— Pies
— Rolls
—
—

Dairy

— Biscuits
— Butter
— Cheese
— Cottage Cheese
— Cream Cheese
— Cream
— Creamer
— Eggs
— Juice
— Margarine
— Milk
— Pudding
— Sour Cream
— Yogurt
—
—

Frozen Foods

— Breakfast
— Dinners
— Ice
— Ice Cream
— Juice
— Pastries
— Pies
— Pizza
— Potatoes
— Vegetables
— Whipping Cream
— Whipped Topping
—
—

Fresh Produce

— Apples
— Avocados
— Bananas
— Beans
— Bell Peppers
— Broccoli
— Cabbage
— Carrots
— Cauliflower
— Celery
— Corn
— Cucumbers
— Garlic
— Grapefruit
— Grapes
— Lemons
— Lettuce
— Lime
— Melons
— Mushrooms
— Onions
— Oranges
— Peaches
— Pears
— Peppers
— Potatoes
— Strawberries
— Spinach
— Squash
— Tomatoes
— Zucchini
—
—

Deli

— Cheese
— Chicken
— Turkey
— Ham
— Main Dish
— Prepared Salad
— Sandwich Meat
— Side Dish
—
—

Grocery List

Grocery

— Beans
— Beer/Wine
— Bread
— Canned Vegetables
—
—
— Cereal
— Chips/Snacks
— Coffee
— Cookies
— Crackers
— Flour
— Honey
— Jelly
— Juice
— Ketchup
— Kool-Aid
— Mayonnaise
— Mixes
—
—
— Mustard
— Nuts/Seeds
— Oil
— Pasta
— Peanut Butter
— Pickles/Olives
— Popcorn
— Rice
— Salad Dressing
— Salt
— Seasonings
—
—
— Sauce
— Sodas
— Soups
— Spices
—
—
— Sugar
— Syrup
— Tea
— Tortillas
— Water
—
—
—

Meat

— Bacon
— Chicken
— Ground Beef
— Ham
—
—
— Hot Dogs
— Pork
— Roast
— Sandwich Meat
— Sausage
— Steak
— Turkey
—
—

General Merchandise

— Automotive
— Baby Items
—
—
— Bath Soap
— Bath Tissue
— Deodorant
— Detergent
— Dish Soap
— Facial Tissue
— Feminine Products
— Aluminum Foil
— Greeting Cards
— Hardware
— Insecticides
— Light Bulbs
— Lotion
— Medicine
— Napkins
— Paper Plates
— Paper Towels
— Pet Supplies
— Prescriptions
— Shampoo
— Toothpaste
— Vitamins
—
—
—

Index

Index

Index

Index

Index

Index

Index

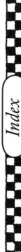

Index

Index

Index

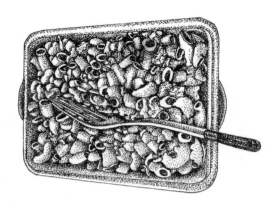

COOKBOOKS PUBLISHED BY COOKBOOK RESOURCES, LLC

The Ultimate Cooking with 4 Ingredients
Easy Cooking with 5 Ingredients
The Best of Cooking with 3 Ingredients
Gourmet Cooking with 5 Ingredients
Healthy Cooking with 4 Ingredients
Diabetic Cooking with 4 Ingredients
4-Ingredient Recipes for 30-Minute Meals
Essential 3-4-5 Ingredient Recipes
The Best 1001 Short, Easy Recipes
Easy Slow-Cooker Cookbook
Essential Slow-Cooker Cooking
Quick Fixes with Cake Mixes
Casseroles to the Rescue
I Ain't On No Diet Cookbook
Kitchen Keepsakes/More Kitchen Keepsakes
Old-Fashioned Cookies
Grandmother's Cookies
Mother's Recipes
Recipe Keepsakes
Cookie Dough Secrets
Gifts for the Cookie Jar
All New Gifts for the Cookie Jar
Gifts in a Pickle Jar
Muffins In A Jar
Brownies In A Jar
Cookie Jar Magic
Easy Desserts
Bake Sale Bestsellers
Quilters' Cooking Companion
Miss Sadie's Southern Cooking
Classic Tex-Mex and Texas Cooking
Classic Southwest Cooking
The Great Canadian Cookbook
The Best of Lone Star Legacy Cookbook
Cookbook 25 Years
Pass the Plate
Texas Longhorn Cookbook
Trophy Hunters' Wild Game Cookbook
Mealtimes and Memories
Holiday Recipes
Little Taste of Texas
Little Taste of Texas II
Texas Peppers
Southwest Sizzler
Southwest Olé
Class Treats
Leaving Home
Easy One-Dish Meals

cookbook resources ® LLC

To Order: **Easy Casseroles Cookbook**

Please send _____ hardcover copies @ $19.95 (U.S.) each $ _____

Texas residents add sales tax @ $1.65 each $ _____

Please send _____ paperback copies @ $16.95 (U.S.) each $ _____

Texas residents add sales tax @ $1.40 each $ _____

Plus postage/handling @ $6.00 (1st copy) $ _____

$1.00 (each additional copy) $ _____

Check or Credit Card (Canada-credit card only) Total $ _____

Charge to: ☐ MasterCard or ☐ VISA

Account # _____

Expiration Date _____

Signature _____

Name _____

Address _____

City _____ State _____ Zip _____

Telephone (day _____ (Evening) _____

Mail or Call:
Cookbook Resources
541 Doubletree Dr.
Highland Village, Texas 75077
Toll Free (866) 229-2665
(972) 317-6404 Fax

To Order: **Easy Casseroles Cookbook**

Please send _____ hardcover copies @ $19.95 (U.S.) each $ _____

Texas residents add sales tax @ $1.65 each $ _____

Please send _____ paperback copies @ $16.95 (U.S.) each $ _____

Texas residents add sales tax @ $1.40 each $ _____

Plus postage/handling @ $6.00 (1st copy) $ _____

$1.00 (each additional copy) $ _____

Check or Credit Card (Canada-credit card only) Total $ _____

Charge to: ☐ MasterCard or ☐ VISA

Account # _____

Expiration Date _____

Signature _____

Name _____

Address _____

City _____ State _____ Zip _____

Telephone (Day) _____ (Evening) _____

Mail or Call:
Cookbook Resources
541 Doubletree Dr.
Highland Village, Texas 75077
Toll Free (866) 229-2665
(972) 317-6404 Fax